I0661845

Benjamin Gough

Lyra Sabbatica

Hymns and poems for Sundays and holy days

Benjamin Gough

Lyra Sabbatica
Hymns and poems for Sundays and holy days

ISBN/EAN: 9783337290269

Printed in Europe, USA, Canada, Australia, Japan

Cover: Foto ©Thomas Meinert / pixelio.de

More available books at **www.hansebooks.com**

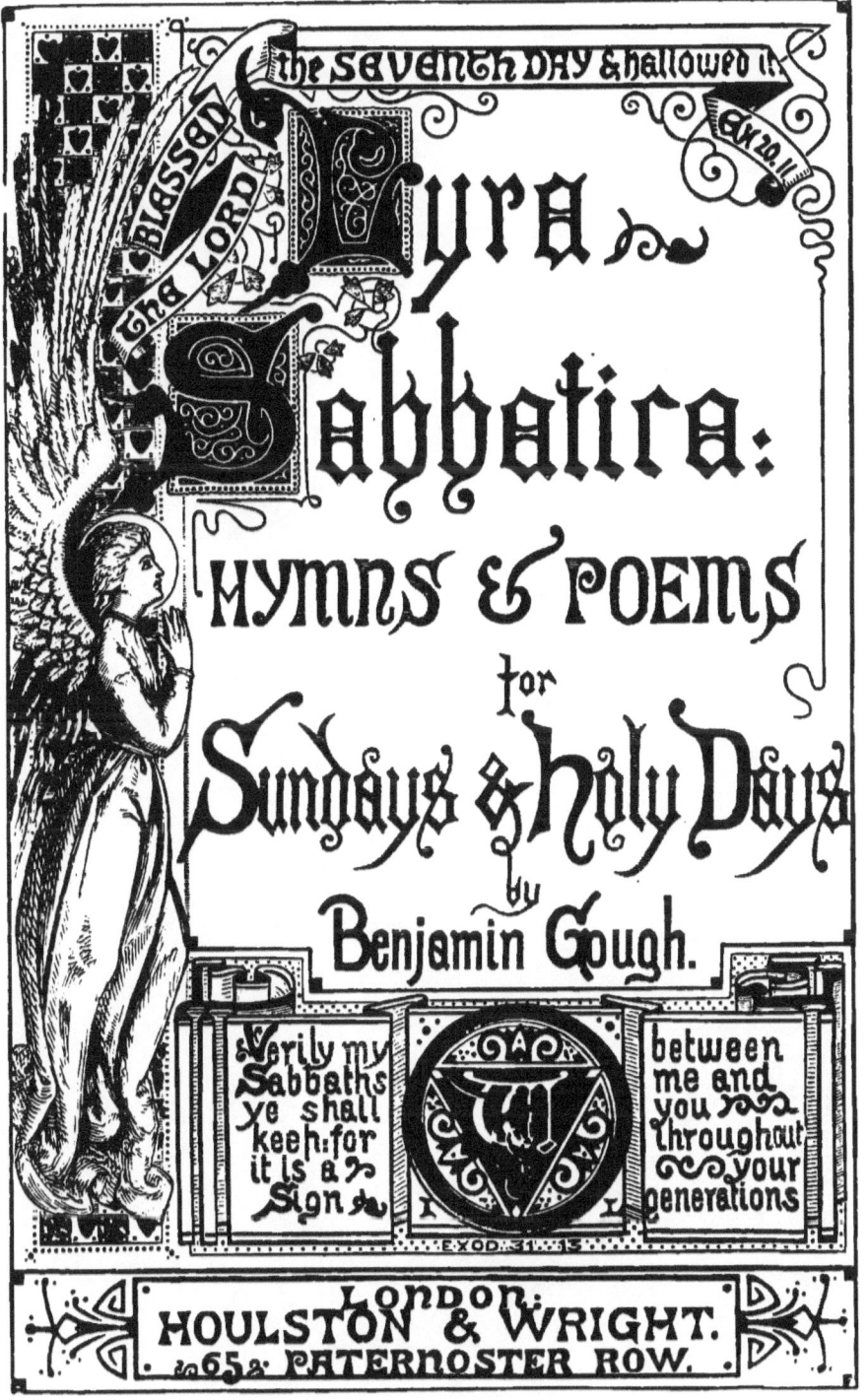

BLESSED the LORD the SEVENTH DAY & hallowed it. Ex 20. 11

Lyra Sabbatica:

HYMNS & POEMS

for

Sundays & Holy Days

by

Benjamin Gough.

Verily my Sabbaths ye shall keeh: for it is a Sign — between me and you throughout your generations

EXOD. 31. 13

London.
HOULSTON & WRIGHT.
65 PATERNOSTER ROW.

LYRA

SABBATICA

HYMNS AND POEMS

FOR

SUNDAYS AND HOLY DAYS

BY

BENJAMIN GOUGH

" LORD, though we change, Thou art the same,
The same sweet God of love and light :
Restore this day, for Thy great Name,
Unto his ancient and miraculous right."

GEORGE HERBERT.

LONDON

HOULSTON & WRIGHT

65, PATERNOSTER ROW

1865.

TO

The Very Rev. Henry Alford, D.D.

DEAN OF CANTERBURY,

WITH PROFOUND RESPECT FOR HIS HIGH MORAL WORTH,

AND LOFTY ATTAINMENTS AS A SCHOLAR,

A THEOLOGIAN, AND A CRITIC,

This Volume

OF

HYMNS AND SACRED POEMS

IS BY PERMISSION

GRATEFULLY DEDICATED.

PREFACE.

THE Author presents this Volume of Sacred Hymns and Poems to the notice of the Public, as a humble Contribution to the accumulating Store of Religious Poetry, the publication of which, as well as its extensive circulation, is a distinguishing and very pleasing Feature of the present Age.

Many of the Poems have appeared in the current Periodicals, but many are entirely new; and it may be said of all, that they breathe a Catholic spirit, exalting Christ as the world's Redeemer, and stimulating to a pure and active Christian life.

The Book, it is believed, may be safely recom-
mended as especially suitable for Sabbath and
Devotional reading, most of the Poems being
founded on Passages or Incidents of Holy
Scripture ; and it is hoped its Songs will add
one more Voice of reverent Exultation to the
grand harmonious Anthem of the universal Church,
—"Glory be to the Father, and to the Son, and
to the Holy Ghost, as it was in the Beginning,
is now, and ever shall be, World without end.
Amen."

Mountfield, near Faversham,
May 1st, 1865.

INDEX OF SUBJECTS.

Index of Subjects. xi

INDEX OF FIRST LINES.

Lyra Sabbatica.

THE SABBATH.

"And He said unto them, That the Son of man is Lord also
of the Sabbath."—St. Luke vi. 5.

SWEET day of rest!
 How pure and quiet is thy dawn;
 How sanctified and blest!
 Softly night's curtain is undrawn,
And holy light comes streaming on the earth,
 Placid and beautifully calm
As that which lit creation's birth
 When the first Sabbath psalm
Rose heavenward on devotion's wings of fire,
And joined the anthems of the Angel-choir.

Sweet day of rest!
We hail thee, brightest of the seven,
 In robes of mercy drest;
Lovely, and full of love, like Heaven.

B

All hallowing influences join.
  Earth's din and toil together cease,
And holy hymn and prayer combine
  To usher in thy peace ;
So like the peace which sin can never break,
Where tears no more are shed, and hearts no more
      shall ache.

      Sweet day of rest !
The Sunday sunshine seems more bright,
  Arrayed in Sabbath vest :
The light is heavenly light.
The hum of bees, the lowing of the herds,
  The streamlet singing through the vale,
The out-door worship of the birds,
  The whisper of the gale,
All rise in concert, sacred and sublime,
Hallowed, and link eternity with time.

      Sweet day of rest !
How doubly sweet thy chiming bells
  Ring out !   God is in quest
Of souls.   His boundless mercy swells
Toward wandering prodigals, to bring them back.
  To-day the Gospel trumpet sounds aloud ;
God's messengers are on our track,
  And the high heavens are bowed
To win and woo our souls to joy and love.
Sweet day of rest ! foretaste of that above.

Sweet day of rest !
Let all with joy "remember" thee,
  And bow to thy behest.
Thou bringest back the songs of jubilee ;
And heavenly freedom smiles on captive men,
  Who spring to angel-life, and rise
To bliss which only angels ken,—
  Communion with the skies!
Sweet day ! sweet Sabbath ! lightened of earth's
  load;
The day was made for man, and man was made
  for God.

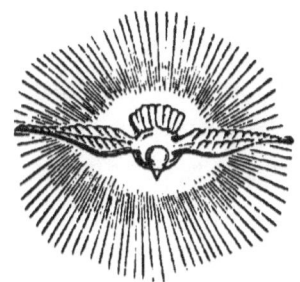

SABBATH MORNING.

"My voice shalt thou hear in the morning, O Lord; in the morning will I direct my prayer unto Thee, and will look up."—PSALM v. 3.

WAKING in the fear of God,
    Upward rise my first desire ;
Upward to the bright abode,
    Upward to the heavenly choir,
Where the saints and angels sing
Praise to Heaven's eternal King.

Upward look my waking eyes,
    Upward tend my longing heart ;
Upward now my prayer shall rise,
    Every want to God impart ;
At the Sabbath's earliest dawn,
Be my soul from earth withdrawn.

Wilt not Thou, my God, supply
    Fully, freely, all my need ;
Listen to my suppliant cry,
    And my utmost thoughts exceed ?
God has promised all I claim—
All I ask in Jesu's name.

Give the Spirit's quickening powers,
  Kindle, Lord, my love and joy;
O how sweet the Sabbath's hours!
  O how blessèd their employ!
Nigh to God if I am found,
Worshipping on holy ground.

Upward, then, I lift my eyes,
  Heavenward springs my loving heart;
Send me Sabbath-day supplies;
  Now the bread of life impart:
Hallowed, then, this day will be,
If I commune, Lord, with Thee.

SABBATH ELEGY IN A COUNTRY
CHURCHYARD.

THE Sabbath bells ring sweetly from
 the tower
  Of the old Church, which on the
  hill-side stands,
And tell, in soft persuasive tones, the hour
 Of prayer, and hymn, and lifting holy hands.

In centuries past, and back to Norman times
 Remote, here has this sanctuary stood ; ·
And buried generations heard the chimes
 On Sabbaths call them to be wise and good.

In yonder porch, in feudal days, the poor
 Met week by week, and friendly converse knew ;
And there, still lingering by the open door,
 Stood youthful groups, beneath the spreading
 yew.

There village maidens, innocent and coy,
 By stalwart swains enamoured, learned to prove
How pure the rapture, and how high the joy,
 The Heaven-inspired emotion of first love.

Barons and Squires, with servitors behind,
   Have paced the open nave in olden days,
And often seen the long procession wind
   To some Gregorian chant of lofty praise.

Those tablets, gnawed by the sharp tooth of Time,
   And shapeless figures—seeming to have grown,
And epitaphs in undeciphered rhyme,
   All dateless now, are history in stone.

In the lone transept, crumbling, bleached, and
     grey,
   A knight in armour lies upon a tomb ;
Perchance a valiant warrior in his day,
   But now forgotten in oblivion's gloom.

Beneath the tower, and crowding either aisle,
   Are mouldering stones, and brasses incomplete,
The broken records of age, name, and style,
   Effaced by time, and the rude peasants' feet.

So fade earth's glories, as a passing dream—
   Substance is only shadow, life a breath—
Like children chasing bubbles on a stream ;
   And serf or noble are alike to Death.

Over the chancel is a window, filled
   With ancient figures and devices quaint ;—
All in dim outline, only half revealed,
   Are holy prophet, seer, and martyred saint.

But chiefly seen, in glory all its own,
   Thorn-crowned, and pierced, and bleeding on
     the tree,
There hangs the world's REDEEMER, and His groan
   Still seems to part His lips in agony.

The blood, fresh flowing from His hands and feet,
   Looks warm with life, while His calm, languid
     eyes
Give utterance of love, and still repeat
   His prayer for blessings on His enemies.

None gaze upon that picture without thought,
   Or meet that pitying glance Divine in vain,
Where God and man, in mystic union brought,
   Show the intensity of love and pain.

So, on Mount Calvary, the Victim hung,
   And the world's sin upon His head was laid ;
Wounded and bruised, with bitter anguish wrung,
   So was the debt of guilty sinners paid.

Around the sacred walls what thousands lie !
   The poor and rich, the righteous and unjust ;
And still accumulating mounds supply
   Ashes to ashes yet, and dust to dust.

The haughty tyrant and the rustic slave,
   Master and servant, here in peace abide ;
The infant hurried to a timeless grave,
   And the hoar patriarch, sleep side by side.

Some new-made graves, bedecked with thyme and
    rose,
    Bespeak that loving hearts are loving still,
And how the mourner's tear of sorrow flows
    In calm submission to Heaven's blessèd will.

On other graves the dust of ages gone
    Has gathered, and no record lives to tell
Their virtues or their crimes, alike unknown,
    Who died ere Wycliffe preached, or Wolsey fell.

O day of unimaginable wonders !
    O time of grandeur—consummation dread !
When the last Judgment, with its world-wide
    thunders,
    Shall bring the Great Assize, and wake the dead !

Star-crowned, fire-robed, and throned on clouds,
    descending
    With holy Angels flaming in His train—
The trumpet-blast of the Archangel rending
    Earth, sea, and sky—Christ shall come down
    again.

O wondrous thought ! O glorious revelation !
    Christ's voice shall drown the din of worldly
    strife ;
The dust of death shall have a new creation,
    And earth's dead millions start again to life.

But now the bells' soft chiming call is ended,
   And the old Church resounds with living voices ;
And many tongues in harmony are blended,
   And many a trembling heart in God rejoices.

Time flies, and generations come and go,
   And change and death assert their gloomy reign :
And still the tide of life shall ebb and flow,
   But God and truth unchangeable remain.

So downwards, until Time's last hour is tolled,
   God's dwelling will be with the meek and mild ;
And evermore the pure in heart shall hold
   Converse with Heaven, in worship undefiled.

THE HOUR OF PRAYER.

"I was glad when they said unto me, Let us go into the house of the Lord. Our feet shall stand within thy gates, O Jerusalem!"—PSALM cxxii. 1, 2.

SWEET is the hour of prayer, and sweet
    the calm
    Sequestered nooks, where Sabbath
    silence reigns;
The whispering breeze is love—the air is balm,
    The sunshine heavenly, and the shady lanes
O'erarched with elms—like some cathedral nave—
    Inspire devotion; while upon the ear
    The swallow's twitter, and the sheep-bell near,
Fall softly, and tall trees in chorus wave,
And Earth in Sabbath smiles, like flowers upon a
    grave.

Sweet is the Sabbath morning, when the chimes
    Ring out their welcome music o'er the land!
Rich music! Gospel call for gospel times,
    Which princes feel, and peasants understand.

What gentle undulations swell and rise,
  Wafted o'er hill and dale, like Mercy's voice;
  Whose loving accents bid our hearts rejoice!
O trembling Prodigal, lift up thine eyes!
O troubled child of God, look upward to the skies!

Come to the house of prayer!   The rich and poor,
  And old and young, together mingle there;
All are alike that pass the Church's door
  To worship God, and join in Common Prayer.
O glorious anthem of ascending praise!
  O deep confession on the bended knee!
  O psalms and hymns of blessèd melody!
O words Divine, to comfort, cheer, and raise
Mourners to wipe their tears, and see their Father's
    face.

Come to the house of prayer! the sacred hour
  Is thine for priceless blessings!   God doth give
Gifts for both worlds to-day—peace, love, and
    power;
  And sends thee strength to die, or grace to live.
Here sounds the Gospel trumpet; here the light
  Of truth for ever shines, a quenchless flame
  On God's high altar; and here Jesu's name
Brings bliss unspeakable—the depth and height
Of love in bounding hearts, who love Him with
    their might.

An hour with God!   O bliss for words too high!
  Foretaste of Heaven!   Epiphany Divine!

O prelude grand of immortality !
O bright rehearsal, ere the choirs shall join
Heaven's Sabbath, and its swell of glory raise !
So doth the Pilgrim Church on earth unite
With ranks triumphant in the realms of light ;
So surely an eternity of praise
Follows sweet hours of prayer, and hallowed Sabbath days.

SABBATH EVENING.

"I will both lay me down in peace, and sleep: for Thou,
Lord, only makest me dwell in safety."—PSALM iv. 8.

BRIGHTLY broke the morning beams
    Of the Sabbath's holy day ;
Now the sunset glory streams,
    And the daylight melts away
Slowly in the western sky,
Tranquil as the zephyr's sigh.

Blessèd has the Sabbath been :
    Matin-song, and evening praise,
From the peasant to the queen,
    Tens of thousands joined to raise.
All their griefs and wants made known ;
Bowed together at the Throne.

Many a troubled heart to-day,
    Many a soul in sorrow sad,
Has found peace and power to pray ;
    God has made His people glad,—
Safe and happy in His care,
Joyful in the house of prayer.

Many a prodigal returned
To his Father's kind embrace,
Has to-day deep lessons learned,
Yielded to the power of grace,
Felt the penitential pain,
Found his Father's house again.

Brightly broke the morning beams ;
Now we hail the Sabbath night.
Hallowed joy and comfort streams,
And at eventide is light.
Calmly now, with thankful breast,
In God's peace we sink to rest.

FOR ANOTHER PENTECOST.

"And it shall come to pass afterward, that I will pour out
My Spirit upon all flesh."—JOEL ii. 28.

QUICKEN, Lord, Thy Church and me;
   Send the promised Spirit down;
Holy One, Eternal Three,
   All Thy former mercies crown:
Father, Son, and Holy Ghost,
Send another Pentecost!

Let the living fire descend,
   Cloven tongues on every head,
Tongues which all may comprehend,—
   Speak Thy life into the dead!
Suddenly the power of grace
Send from Heaven, and fill the place.

Send the rushing. mighty wind,
   Give the utterance Divine;
Let us know the Spirit's mind;
   Let us speak in words of Thine:
Send a pure baptismal shower,—
Tongues of fire, and words of power.

Lyra Sabbatica.

As of old, so be it now,
  Now the glorious scene repeat ;
See Thy humbled people bow,
  Waiting lowly at Thy feet,
Crying all with one accord,
Send the promised Spirit, Lord !

First on the believing few,
  Then in widening power unfurled ;
Gathering, as the Deluge grew,
  Pour Thy Spirit on the world ;
Bright in panoply Divine,
Bid Thy Church arise and shine.

Jesus ! glorious Victor, come,
  Thou whose right it is to reign ;
Call Thine ancient people home,
  Paradise restore again :
Father, Son, and Holy Ghost,
Send another Pentecost !

FOR THE FORTY DAYS OF LENT.

" And rend your heart, and not your garments, and turn
unto the Lord your God: for He is gracious and merciful,
slow to anger, and of great kindness, and repenteth Him of
the evil."—JOEL ii. 13.

HY lies the Church in sackcloth,
    and her hymns
    And joyous anthems hushed in
    solemn pause,
And ashes on her head her beauty dims,
    And, shrinking from earth's glare and vain
    applause,
    For forty days to solitude withdraws ?
Ask not for why,—with tremulous steps and slow
    She follows Him she loves, to love yet more,
And seeks the lonely wilderness, to know
    More of His heart's deep love than e'er she
    knew before.

There, in prostration at the Master's feet,
    She drops the tears of penitence alone,
Embracing while she weeps, with reverence meet,—
    " Thy faithless Bride, though faithless yet Thine
    own,
    Cast not away, nor let Thy gathering frown.

Rise into judgment; spare Thy people, Lord!
Shall Satan triumph where Thy Cross hath stood?
Speak to Thine heritage some peaceful word;
    And comfort still Thy Church, bought with
    Thine own dear Blood."

She mourns defilement in her holiest things :
    Alas! too oft her altar-fires have waned,
And worldly love held back her buoyant wings;
    Her songs all heartless, and her prayers re-
    strained,
    And her twin sacraments by evil stained.
Her Captain always conquers, but in fear
    She hides the Cross, and drops the Spirit's sword;
Yet now in meek abasement she draws near,
    And girds herself afresh to battle for her Lord,

Who fought for her and triumphed; all His foes
    And ours lay vanquished at His conquering feet;
Pain, sickness, death, and sin's unnumbered woes,
    And Satan, in his wilderness retreat,
    And earth, and hell, to Him pay homage meet.
Strength triumphed in His weakness, life in death :
    On the cold ground, in dark Gethsemane,
And on the bloody Cross, the Conqueror's wreath
    Blooms on His fainting brow, in sign of victory.

And shall Thy humbled Church in vain desire
    Pardon and quickening from her living Head?
Wilt Thou not send the Pentecostal fire,
    And give again the flaming tongues, to spread
    The Gospel message, life unto the dead?

O bid the sacramental host arise,
   Fair as the moon, and brighter than the sun,
And like a bannered army, rend the skies
   With mingled shout and prayer, till earth to
   Christ is won.

Sweet is the 'plaining of a contrite heart,
   And welcome is the incense of its sighs
To Him we love ; and sweet t' Him to impart
   Pardon and joy, and wipe the weeper's eyes ;
   Before His loving voice all sorrow flies.
So, from the wilderness, the Church returns,
   Leaning on her Belovèd, clothed in light,
His spotless Bride ; and now she only burns
   To win the world to Him, and conquer in His
   might.

.

PLEASURES FOR EVERMORE.

"Thou wilt show me the path of life: in Thy presence is fulness of joy; at Thy right hand there are pleasures for ever-more."—PSALM xvi. 11.

PLEASURES for evermore
  At God's right hand;
  Fulness of joy in store
   In that bright land.
Yonder in Heaven I see
A place prepared for me ;
And my glory doth rejoice,
While I sing with heart and voice,
Come to that heavenly rest,
 Give all thy wanderings o'er
Come, share among the blest,
 Pleasures for evermore !

O God ! 'midst worldly strife
 Maintain my lot;
Show me the path of life,—
 Thou changest not.
O bid my heart be glad,
And my soul in sunshine clad ;

Let my flesh in hope repose,
Till the blast of Judgment blows,
Then breaks the endless Day —
    Shout, triumph, and adore ;
To the haven of joy away,
    Pleasures for evermore !

Gird up thy loins and run,
    Eternal life to gain ;
Now is the race begun ;
    Run not in vain.
To His blest sceptre bow ;
O come to Jesus now ;
Let thy faith be fixed on Him,
Till with radiant cherubim
Thou shalt join the glorious throng,
    And tread the golden floor,
And eternally prolong
    Pleasures for evermore !

HOW BEAUTEOUS ON THE MOUNTAINS.

"How beautiful upon the mountains are the feet of Him that bringeth good tidings, that publisheth peace; that bringeth good tidings of good, that publisheth salvation; that saith unto Zion, Thy God reigneth!"—ISAIAH lii. 7.

NOW beauteous on the mountains
   Are the feet of Him that brings,
Like streams from living fountains,
   Good tidings of good things!
That publisheth salvation,
   And jubilee release,
To every tribe and nation,
   God's reign of joy and peace.

Lift up thy voice, O watchmen!
   And shout from Zion's towers
Thy hallelujah chorus,
   "The victory is ours!"
The Lord shall build up Zion
   In glory and renown,
And Jesus, Judah's Lion,
   Shall wear His rightful crown.

Break forth in hymns of gladness,
  O waste Jerusalem !
Let songs, instead of sadness,
  Thy jubilee proclaim.
The Lord, in strength victorious,
  Upon thy foes hath trod ;
Behold, O earth ! the glorious
  Salvation of our God !

Go forth in strength and glory,
  Ye heralds of the Cross,
And blow the Gospel trumpet,
  And fight for Jesus' cause.
Each man with fiery censer,
  Each heart with love Divine,
Burning with flame intenser,
  Like the seraphim to shine.

So shall earth's many nations
  Be sprinkled with THE BLOOD ;
So, in bright revelations,
  The Spirit be bestowed.
Thy reign millennial hasten,
  O Christ ! Thy sceptre sway,—
Till then our joys we chasten,
  Till then we watch and pray.

NO CONDEMNATION.

"There is therefore now no condemnation to them which are in Christ Jesus, who walk not after the flesh, but after the Spirit."—ROMANS viii. 1.

THERE is no condemnation,
  But peace and joy unpriced,
  And full and free salvation
    To all that are in Christ;
The sinner, broken-hearted,
  In penitential tears,
Has joy and peace imparted
  As soon as Christ appears.

The law of life in Jesus,
  The Spirit's power within,
This only can release us,
  And break and cancel sin;
The Spirit and the Blood
  Received by simple faith,
And then we rise renewed,
  And conquer sin and death.

Made free from condemnation,
　And Jesus all our own,
In Him we have salvation,
　We trust in Him alone ;
And walking in the Spirit,
　Into new life we rise,
And, heirs with Christ, inherit
　A mansion in the skies.

THE MARTYRDOM OF ST. STEPHEN.

"And they stoned Stephen, calling upon God, and saying, Lord Jesus, receive my spirit. And he kneeled down, and cried with a loud voice, Lord, lay not this sin to their charge. And when he had said this, he fell asleep."—ACTS vii. 59, 60.

EFORE the Jews' Sanhedrim
Stood Stephen the Evangel,
And his calm face shone forth with grace
Celestial, like an Angel.
Around his head a halo spread,
With Heaven's own radiance glorious;
A martyr-crown, by Christ sent down,
To make his death victorious.

O for a limner's pencil,
Or sculptor's inspiration!
A Seraph's tongue might swell the song
Of Stephen's exaltation.
Unmoved and fearless, firm and tearless,
'Midst scorning and derision,
Earth's veil was riven, and open Heaven
Burst on his raptured vision.

O soul-entrancing wonder!
Transporting revelation!
With upturned gaze, in meek amaze
And awe-struck contemplation,

Heaven's golden light flamed on his sight,
  Its portals wide expanding,
And God's high throne in splendour shone,
  With Christ in glory standing.

Then came the hour of terror,
  The martyr's bitter anguish :
Cast out and stoned, in pangs he groaned ;
  All friendless left to languish,
While cruel cries of foes arise
  From loud and many voices :
With fiendish speed the bloody deed
  Is done, and Hell rejoices.

Christ's martyr, all triumphant,
  Dies while on Jesus calling ;
And prays for those his murderous foes,
  While the rough stones are falling.
O courage bold ! O love untold !
  Such agony enduring ;
First on the roll of Christ's red scroll
  The martyr's crown securing.

Kneel down, O noble martyr !
  Through Christ thy Master's merit
To Heaven ascending, with Angels blending,
  God will receive thy spirit !
Firmly relying, gently dying,
  In sweet and placid slumber,
Now swell Heaven's song, and join the throng
  Which none on earth can number.

WELLS OF SALVATION.

ISAIAH xii.

LORD I will praise Thee, and sing,
　　Exulting with joy and delight,
O'ershadowed by Mercy's broad wing,
　　And shielded by day and by night.
Though once Thou wast angry with me,
　　Thine anger is now turned away ;
Thy reconciled face 1 can see ;
　　Thy word is my comfort and stay.

The God of salvation is mine ;
　　Never more will I be afraid,
But trust in His favour Divine,
　　And rest, on His faithfulness stayed.
The Lord is my strength and my song,
　　My heart shall rejoice in His love ;
Till I join the glorified throng,
　　And praise Him for ever above.

And therefore my daily employ
　　Is to draw, 'mid confusion and strife,
From wells of salvation, with joy,
　　The beautiful waters of life ;

And filled with the spirit of peace,
  In harmony's sweetest accord,
My raptures shall daily increase,
  Ineffably one with my Lord.

O Zion ! in anthems unite
  To Jesus thy glory and crown,
Who reigns in omnipotent might,
  And dwells in the midst of His own.
Thy Holy One, Israel, is great ;
  And all who in Jesus abide
Are safe, while they patiently wait
  Till the Bridegroom shall come for the Bride.

THE KINGDOM OF HEAVEN TAKEN BY FORCE.

ST. MATTHEW xi. 12.

OME ye who enquire, with earnest desire,
  For pardon and peace,
And long from your sins a speedy release,

Still mightily cry, till Jesus draw nigh
  To the penitent soul,
At once by the balm of Gilead made whole.

Never yield to despair! Be importunate prayer
  Your only resource ;
The Kingdom of Heaven is taken by force.

By the power from on high, believingly cry
  Through the Covenant Blood,—
The life-giving stream, which on Calvary flowed :

The Kingdom of Heaven to him shall be given
  Who in violent groans
Pleads the promise of God, and the Blood which atones.

Come, sinner, just now in penitence bow ;
  And the Kingdom of Heaven,
With Jesus, and pardon in Him, shall be given.

AS THE PANTING HART DESIRES.

Psalm xlii.

As the panting hart desires
    The cooling water-brooks,
So, O God, my soul aspires
    To Thee, and heavenward looks,
Thirsting for the living God.
    When, O when shall I appear,
Joyful in Thy bright abode,
    And with Thy saints draw near?

Tears have been my constant meat,
    And sorrow, day and night:
All mine enemies are great;
    My grief is their delight.
Like the roaring of a flood
    Deep calleth unto deep around;
Yet my hope is fixed on God,
    In Him my help is found.

O my God! my troubled soul
    Within me is cast down;
Billows of affliction roll
    Like water·spouts to drown!

Yet will I look up to Thee,
   And call to mind Thy mercy still;
Jordan shall remembered be,
   And Mizar's holy hill.

Thou, my God, wilt still command
   Thy kindness day by day;
Hold me by Thy mighty hand,
   Thy love my only stay :
In the night of deepest gloom
   Songs shall rise to God on high,
And my prayer, like sweet perfume,
   Ascend beyond the sky.

Why art thou cast down, my soul,
   Disquieted within ?
Strong in Christ, thy foes control,
   And conquer every sin !
Hope in God, and praise His name;
   Victor thou through Jesu's blood,
None shall put thy soul to shame,
   Or shake thy trust in God.

SLEEPING AND WAKING.

" For so He giveth His beloved sleep."—Psalm cxxvii. 2.
"When I awake, I am still with Thee."—Psalm cxxxix.
18.

THEY only know the true repose of
  sleep
   Who rest in God,
  Within the fold, among the chosen
  sheep;
Them the Good Shepherd evermore doth keep,
  With crook and rod.
 With minds serenely calm,
 And holy hymn or psalm,
 Sleep's gentle, healing balm
Steals softly o'er them in a dream of love,
 While Heaven's own music charms,
  And they lie down to prove
   Peace from above.
 And so, reclining in their Shepherd's arms,
They rest securely, Jesu's sheep,
" For so He giveth His belovèd sleep."

Sleep is not sloth, nor dull forgetfulness ;
    Who sleep in God,
Their rest is holy, Angels come to bless,
And their own sanctities of thought impress,
    And shed abroad
  Odours like incense sweet,
  Until in dreams we meet
  Loved ones in bliss to greet,
And hear the whispers of our Father's voice
    In tenderness Divine.
  Then faith is turned to sight,
And while we slumber, we rejoice
    Their ranks to join,
And such high company to keep,—
" For so He giveth His belovèd sleep."

Sleep is not long. We wake, for day is here ;
    But still with God.
Sleeping or waking, God is ever near ;
We grasp His hand, like children all in fear,
    Along life's road ;
  And still secure abide
  Close to our Father's side,
  Whatever may betide ;
And not more brightly doth the morning sun
  Shine in the latticed room,
    Proclaiming day begun,
  And scattering night's gloom,

Than doth God's loving sunshine fall on me,
While with glad heart I bow the reverent knee :
Sleeping or waking, " I am still with Thee."

Sleep in the grave is hallowed, and our rest
　　　Is sleep in God.
Calmly we lie down on our Father's breast,
　His holy arm around us prest,
　　　In Death's abode ;
　And ever, through the night,
　We wait the morning's light,
　Gloriously bright,
Bursting in splendour from the flaming sky,
　To the loud trumpet-blast
　　Of resurrection nigh.
　Earth all ablaze we see, and Hell aghast,
And Christ, cloud-throned, descending from on
　　　high ;—
O rapturous waking ! when from death set free,
Thou, Thou, my God, art nigh, and " I am still
　　　with Thee."

TO AN AFFLICTED CHILD.

[ONE OF CHRIST'S LAMBS, SINCE GATHERED INTO
THE HEAVENLY FOLD.]

GENTLEST lamb of Jesu's fold,
    Called to suffer from thy birth,
Take of Heaven a firmer hold,
    Since thou art not made for earth ;
Only lie at Jesu's feet,
Then affliction will be sweet.

Clasp thy tiny hands in prayer,
    Tell the Saviour all thy heart,
Trust Him with thy every care,
    Every grief to Him impart ;
Bow to Him the suppliant knee,
Once He was a child like thee.

Take thy refuge in His arms,
    Nestle in His loving breast,
Fly to Him in all alarms,
    Fly for safety, peace, and rest.
Weep not, darling, at His will,
Love Him, trust Him, praise Him still.

Meekly learn thy cross to bear,
    Never murmur or complain,
Cheerful songs and holy prayer
    Ease and sanctify thy pain.
Sing of Jesus and His love,—
So the angels sing above.

Gentlest lamb of Jesu's fold,
    Called to suffer from thy birth,
Take of Heaven a firmer hold,
    Since thou art not made for earth ;
Only lie at Jesu's feet,
Then affliction will be sweet.

FOR SATURDAY NIGHT.

" And Joshua said unto the people, Sanctify yourselves:
for to-morrow the Lord will do wonders among you."—
JOSHUA iii. |5.|

CHAFED and worn with worldly care,
Sweetly, Lord, my heart prepare ;
Bid this inward tempest cease ;
Jesus, come and whisper peace.
Hush the whirlwind of my will,
With Thyself my spirit fill ;
End in calm this busy week,
Let the Sabbath gently break.

Sever, Lord, these earthly ties,
Fain my soul to Thee would rise ;
Disentangle me from time,
Lift me to a purer clime,
Let me cast away my load,
Let me now draw nigh to God ;
Gently, loving Jesus, speak,
End in calm this busy week.

Draw the curtain of repose
While my wearied eyelids close ;
Seal my spirit while I rest,
Give me dreamings pure and blest.
Raise me with a cheerful heart;
Holy Ghost, Thyself impart,
Then the Sabbath day will be
Heaven brought down to earth and me.

FEAR NOT, O JACOB.

" Fear not, O Jacob, My servant; and thou, Jesurun, whom I
have chosen."—ISAIAH xliv. 2.

HUS saith the Lord that made thee,
   And formed thee for His glory,—
    O Israel, hear ! why shouldst thou fear ?
   Thy God shall go before thee.
O Jacob and Jesurun !
   No longer yield to sadness,
Thy faithful Lord fulfils His word,
   And turns thy grief to gladness.

According to His promise,
   He breaks our bonds asunder,
His love imparts, and fills our hearts
   With mingled joy and wonder;
The clouds that darkly threatened,
   And hung impending o'er us,
Melt into light, and Heaven grows bright,
   And Canaan smiles before us.

And teeming showers of blessing,
   The waters of salvation,
Come freely down, our bliss to crown,
   And swell our exultation ;

Waters on him that's thirsty
   In streams of life are pouring,
Floods on dry ground are all around,
   Beauty and life restoring.

O plenitude of mercy!
   O world-convincing Spirit!
For us blood-bought, and given when sought,
   Through Jesu's dying merit;
As in days Pentecostal,
   In might and triumph glorious,
O come again, till Jesus reign
   In every heart victorious!

Haste, haste, bright day of glory!
   Long-promised, dawning slowly;
Jesus, arise! and gild the skies
   With Thy millennium holy!
Come to Thy Bride, O Bridegroom!
   In union none can sever;
Thine, Thine alone, till round Thy Throne
   We praise Thy name for ever.

ONE SHALL SAY, I AM THE LORD'S.

ISAIAH xliv. 5.

I AM the Lord's,
 Henceforth, for ever;
Soul and body, deeds and words,
 All I have, and all I am,
Yielding to His rightful claim :
 Nor Earth nor Hell shall sever,
Now the Book of Life records
 I am the Lord's.

I am the Lord's
 Through Jesu's merit ;
Bind the sacrifice with cords
 To the altar of the Cross.
Now I count all things but loss,
 And yielding to the Spirit,
Watch and wait for Heaven's rewards ;
 I am the Lord's.

I am the Lord's.
 For ever cleaving,
With the Lord's my will accords,
 Loving, gentle, self-subdued,

Washed in the atoning blood ;
  All humble, all believing.
O the rapture this affords !
  I am the Lord's !

I am the Lord's ;
  This watchword glorious
Clears my way like flaming swords ;
  Satan, sin, and death o'ercome,
Soon I reach my heavenly home,
  Eternally victorious :
Angels ! strike your loftiest chords !
  I am the Lord's !

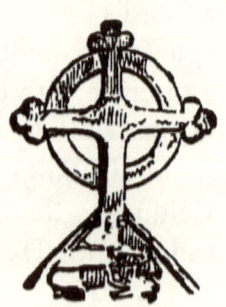

PRAISE YE THE LORD!

PSALMS cxlviii., cl.

PRAISE the Lord from Heaven's
   height,
  Where holy angels dwell;
  Sun, and moon, and stars of light,
Your mighty chorus swell ;
With thy million tongues, O earth,
  Join the anthem as it sweeps
In its majesty of mirth ;
  Join, ye dragons, and all deeps,
Fire and hail, and snow and wind;
  Swell thy bass, O rushing storms ;
Loosened thunders, now unbind
  Melody's most awful forms ;
Mountains and all hills, break forth,
East and west, and south and north;
Fruitful trees, and cedars tall,
  Birds, and beasts, and creeping things,
Join the hallelujah call,
  Worship now the King of kings ;
Lakes and rivers, clear and bright,
Oceans fathomless, unite :
Solemnly, with one accord,
Praise and magnify the Lord.

Kings and princes of the earth,
 Judges in your seats of power,
Young men in your pride of birth,
 Maidens in your youthful hour,
Old men verging on the tomb,
 Let your tremulous voices rise ;
Children, in your youthful bloom,
 Praise the Lord of earth and skies ;
All that breathe the breath of life,
 Shout or sweep the harmonious chord,
Emulate in hallowed strife
 Who shall best His name record.
Let the earth, with anthems rife,
 Praise and magnify the Lord.

In the solemn temple choir,
 Where the multitudes unite,
Where the holy altar-fire
 Quenchless burns by day and night ;
In His firmament of power,
 Where the heavens lie spread abroad,
Uttering praises every hour,
 Join in glorifying God.

All in earth and heaven assembling ;
Angels bowing,—mortals trembling ;
Praise the Lord of earth and sky,
He who gave His Son to die ;
He whose mighty acts and deeds
All our highest thought exceeds.

Praise Him with the trumpet's sound,
  Psaltery and lute, awake !
Miriam's timbrel now be found ;
  David's harp, sweet music make;
Stringèd instruments resound
Melodies till now unknown ;
  Organs, join the solemn shout ;
  Cymbals, loud in songs break out,
Lift your anthems to the throne :
Earth and Heaven, with one accord,
Laud and magnify the Lord.

THE REIGN OF CHRIST.

"Behold, a King shall reign in righteousness."—ISA. xxxii. 1.

JESUS, our victorious King,
    Shall reign in righteousness ;
Peace and joy His rule shall bring,
    And every nation bless.
He shall be a hiding-place,
    A covert rock of shelter stand ;
Streams of never-failing grace
    Shall flow in every land.

All the kingdoms of the earth
    To Him shall homage pay ;
Chant in songs His royal birth,
    And own His sovereign sway :
Kings bow down before His throne,
    And lowly worship at His feet ;
Heathen nations, yet unknown,
    With hallelujahs greet.

Then the Spirit from above
    Shall on the earth be poured ;
Every heart be filled with love,
    And paradise restored.

Upon every fruitful field
  God shall send a large increase ;
And the ransomed world shall yield
  The Harvest-Home of peace.

Judgment in the wilderness
  Shall then delight to dwell,
And the fruits of righteousness
  In glorious clusters swell ;
Quiet in unruffled joy
  Then the Church shall calmly rest,
Praising Jesus her employ,
  And leaning on His breast.

E

CHRIST IN SIMON'S HOUSE.

"And one of the Pharisees desired Him that He would
eat with him. And He went into the Pharisee's house, and
sat down to meat."—St. Luke vii. 36.

A T Bethany, in Simon's house,
    Sat Jesus down to meat,
In royal condescension
    And tender love, most sweet :
Not for His pleasure went He
    To join that festive board,
But that one mourning wanderer
    From God might be restored.

A woman in the city,
    And she a sinner, came,—
An uninvited guest was she,
    Impelled by guilt and shame ;
Behind His feet she stood abashed
    In sorrow keen and deep ;
No word the trembling mourner said,
    But there she stood to weep.

O welcome, stricken one, art thou,
  With all thy sins and fears,—
A sinner with a broken heart,
  A sinner in her tears.
There weeping at His feet abide,
  And humbly wait His will,
For He, whose name is Jesus,
  Receiveth sinners still.

A box of alabaster
  She holdeth in her hands,
Of ointment very precious,
  And scents from many lands.
With tears she washed His sacred feet,
  And wiped them with her hair;
And kissed His feet with reverence meet,
  And broke the ointment there.

O sharp, inwrought contrition,
  Which sorrowing sinners prove!
O sweet and fragrant offering,
  Which speaks her heart's deep love!
O joy, to weep in sorrow
  For sins of by-gone years!
O blessèd grief, which brings relief
  In penitential tears!

Arise, thou fallen weeper!
  Thou wounded one, heart-riven
With anguish sore, O weep no more;
  Thy sins are all forgiven!

The sighing of the contrite
   Brings ever sure release;
What joy awakes when Jesus speaks,
   And bids thee go in peace !

So, henceforth and for ever,
   Where'er the Gospel comes,
The offering of this woman
   Shall shed its rich perfumes ;
And stand Christ's own memorial stone,
   A record high and true,
That all mankind through Him may find
   A present pardon too.

THE ACCEPTABLE FAST.

"Is not this the fast that I have chosen? to loose the bands of wickedness, to undo the heavy burdens, and to let the oppressed go free, and that ye break every yoke?"— ISAIAH lviii. 6.

NOT clothed in sackcloth, and in ashes lying,
    With heads downcast,
But hearts all blackened with the Devil's dyeing,
And lives of shameless lust, God's law defying :
    Not thus we fast.

Not with mock sorrow to afflict our souls
    For evils past,
While yet our sin as a sweet morsel rolls
Under our tongue, and all our life controls :
    Not thus we fast.

Not seeing first our humble brother's " mote,"
    And our " beam " last ;
Not for debate, or strife, or worldly note,
While taking our poor neighbour by the throat :
    Not thus we fast.

Not in the Church, long-faced, in unctuous qualms
    By none surpassed,
Reciting the seven penitential psalms

With perjured lips unclean, and fraud-stained
    palms:
      Not thus we fast.

This is God's fast, acceptable and true ;—
      A good repast
Given to the hungry, while thy hands undo
The yoke, and give th' oppressed their due :
      This is God's fast.

To loose the bands of slavery and wrong
      By tyrants cast ;
To bring into thine house the outcast throng,
And tune the widow's sorrowing heart to song :
      This is God's fast.

In dens and rookeries of filth and sin,
      In cities vast,
To find a brother, and by kindness win
Him back to God and manhood as thy kin :
      This is God's fast.

God's fasts are feasts, and " Give ye them to eat "
      Stands to the last.
Not your cold homily they want, but meat ;
Food first, and then the sermon to complete :
      This is God's fast.

So shall thy light shine forth as morning's glory
      When night is past ;
And wealth and righteousness shall go before thee,
And God shall spare thee till thy head is hoary :
      This is God's fast.

WHY DO THE HEATHEN RAGE?

"Why do the heathen rage, and the people imagine a vain thing? The kings of the earth set themselves, and the rulers take counsel together, against the Lord, and against His Anointed."—PSALM ii. 1, 2.

HY do the heathen rage,
  And earth and hell engage?
  Counsel take against the Lord,
  His Anointed to o'erthrow?
Jesus, God's eternal Son,
  Lives to conquer every foe.

Rulers and kings allied,
  Vain is their impious pride;
He, the King in Bethlehem born,
  Sitting now enthroned on high,
He shall laugh them all to scorn;
  He shall gain the victory.

High on God's holy hill
  He executes His will;
Jesus sways the sceptre there,
  King of saints by sovereign right,
Makes His Church His royal care,
  Shields His people day and night.

Hail ! glorious reign begun !
God's everlasting Son,
O fulfil the great decree !
Father ! hear the Church's prayer !
Let the heathen nations see
Jesu's mighty arm made bare.

O let the world bow down,
Jesus the King to crown ;
Every foe to Him submit,
Conquered by His dying love ;
Drawn, and humbled at His feet,
By the Spirit from above.

Sinners to Jesus won,
Kneel down and kiss the Son ;
Pardon, peace, and joy, and Heaven,
Come through Jesu's blood alone :
O believe and be forgiven,
Make the blessing now your own !

FLOODS ON THE DRY GROUND.

" For I will pour water upon him that is thirsty, and floods
upon the dry ground."—ISAIAH xliv. 3.

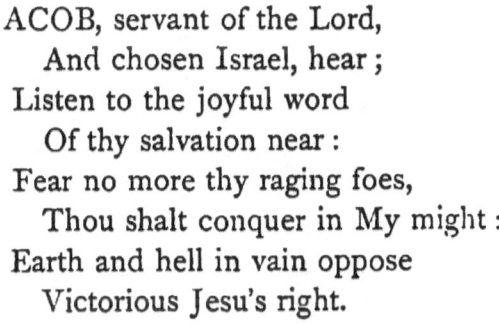

ACOB, servant of the Lord,
  And chosen Israel, hear ;
Listen to the joyful word
  Of thy salvation near :
Fear no more thy raging foes,
  Thou shalt conquer in My might :
Earth and hell in vain oppose
  Victorious Jesu's right.

Water on the thirsty poor,
  And floods on the dry ground,
I, the Lord thy God, will pour,
  Till fruitful streams abound :
Upon all My ransomed seed
  I will send My Spirit down ;
All thine offspring, blest indeed,
  Shall wear the victor's crown.

Springing up by Zion's fords,
  Like willows by a brook,
" One shall say, I am the Lord's,"
  And toward His altar look ;

Others shall lift up their hands,
    And Israel's name and glory take ;
Join them to Immanuel's bands,
    And fight for Jesu's sake.

Hasten, Lord, the Joyful Day ;
    Fulfil Thy word, fulfil ;
Pour Thy Spirit out, we pray,
    And bless Thy Israel still.
Crown Thy ministers with fire,
    And honour still the Gospel word ;
Souls by millions be their hire,
    Who preach our conquering Lord.

Glorious Gospel ! spread and grow !
    Fly on the wings of light !
Until all mankind shall know
    And worship God aright ;
Until every knee shall bow,
    And Jesus every tongue confess.
Hail, Immanuel ! triumph now,
    And now the nations bless.

STREAMS IN THE DESERT.

"In the wilderness shall waters break out, and streams in the desert."—ISAIAH xxxv. 6.

IN the lonely wilderness
   And solitary place,
Jesus, make them glad, and bless
   With Thy refreshing grace.
Bid Thy banished ones rejoice ;
   Hidden springs of life disclose ;
Let the deserts hear Thy voice,
   And blossom as the rose.

On the heights of Lebanon,
   O let Thy presence shine !
Carmel's mount and Sharon own
   The excellence Divine :
Let the heathen tribes behold,
   And Jesus hail with one accord ;
Unto all mankind unfold
   The glory of the Lord.

Let the weakened hands be strong,
   Confirm the feeble knees :
O ye dumb ! break forth in song ;
   Ye troubled hearts, find ease.

End the years of parching drought,
　And streams into the desert send :
O ye water-springs ! gush out ;
　Ye heavenly rains, descend !

Let the ransomed of the Lord
　With songs to Zion come ;
Now be Paradise restored
　In every heart and home ;
Joy and gladness fill the earth ;
　Hasten, bright millennial Day !
Everlasting songs of mirth,
　And sorrow fled away.

Walking in the King's highway
　Of holiness and love,
Then the Church on earth shall pray
　And praise like that above ;
Until Jesus rend the sky,
　And come to claim His spotless Bride,
Lift her to His throne on high,
　And seat her at His side.

WHY ART THOU CAST DOWN?

"Why art thou cast down, O my soul? and why art thou disquieted within me? hope thou in God: for I shall yet praise Him, who is the health of my countenance, and my God."—PSALM xlii. 11.

S the hart panteth for water-brooks
 clear,
 So my soul fainteth, till Jesus draw
 near:
All is sorrow and gloom; I groan under my load;
O when shall I come and appear before God?

My tears are my meat; day and night do I mourn,
For mercy entreat, and for God to return:
My soul is cast down, and my heart is in pain,
Nor, till God is made known, can I comfort regain.

Deep calleth to deep, while rough billows and
 waves
Wildly over me sweep, and the hurricane raves;
Loud water-spouts roar, and, like swords in my
 bones,
My foes evermore still laugh at my moans.

Yet will I arise and look to the Lord,
And lift up mine eyes, and rest on His Word ;
From Jordan's sweet stream, and Mizar's green hill
Remember His name, and rejoice in Him still.

For the Lord will command loving-kindness and
     peace,
And guide by His hand, and His mercy increase :
By day and by night, amid sorrow and strife,
My prayer I'll indite to the God of my life.

Why art thou cast down, O disquieted soul ?
Though thine enemies frown, and storm-billows
     roll,
Praise God evermore for mercies bestowed ;
Love, trust, and adore Him, thy health and thy
     God.

THE GOSPEL MESSAGE.

"And He said unto them, Go ye into all the world, and preach the Gospel to every creature."—ST. MARK xvi. 15.

O ye into all the world,
  And preach the Gospel word ;
  Jesu's banner be unfurled,
   The everlasting Lord !
Tell to every nation, tell
  The year of Jubilee is come ;
Snatch the prodigal from hell,
  And call the exile home.

In the Spirit's power and might,
  The heathen millions claim ;
Claim them as His royal right,
  In Jesu's conquering name,—
His inheritance of old,
  Though the foe has long withstood,—
With His ransomed ones enrolled,
  And purchased with His blood.

Raise the song of Jubilee,
  And let the trumpet sound ;
Bid the captive ones go free,
  With hallowed gladness crowned.

Cry aloud, and shout for joy,
  Publish peace for all mankind ;
Happiness without alloy,
  Which all who seek may find.

Chosen messengers, go forth,
  And bear the news of grace,
East, and west, and south, and north,
  To all the human race :
Fired with zeal and heavenly love,
  Ambassadors of Christ, arise !
Filled with unction from above,
  To preach and to baptize.

Go forth, bearing precious seed,
  And weeping as ye go ;
Surely shall your work succeed,
  And every seed shall grow.
Doubtless shall ye come again,
  When your day of toil is past,
Shouting, with your golden grain,
  The Harvest-Home at last !

SING WE MERRILY TO GOD.

"O sing unto the Lord a new song; for He hath done
marvellous things."—PSALM xcviii. 1.

ING we merrily to God
  A new triumphant song;
Worship toward His bright abode,
  With joyful heart and tongue :
Sing with harps unto the Lord,
  With cornets' and with trumpets' sound;
All the earth, with one accord,
  Jehovah's praise resound.

His right hand and holy arm,
  Omnipotently nigh,
Shields His saints from every harm,
  And gives the victory.
Marvellous in power and love
  Are the things which God hath done;
All mankind His goodness prove,
  Who gave His only Son.

He, His mercy and His grace
  Remembering evermore,
Dwells in every holy place,
  To show His saving power:

F

In the heathen's sight displayed,
  His salvation is made known ;
There is daily worship paid,
  And there is Jesu's throne.

Clap your hands, ye rolling floods,
  And thou, O ocean, roar !
Wave in concert, O ye woods !
  Ye mountain heights, adore !
Shout in joy before the Lord,
  Who comes in righteousness to reign !
Shout for Paradise restored,
  And love to God and man !

Sing we merrily to God,
  And make a joyful noise ;
Angels, from your high abode,
  O swell the mighty voice !
Sound His praise from pole to pole,
  Over continent and sea ;
Let the rapturous pæan roll
  To all Eternity !

ALL OVER THE WORLD.

"But in the last days it shall come to pass, that the mountain of the house of the Lord shall be established in the top of the mountains."—MICAH iv. 1.

LL over the world be Thy banner
    unfurled,
        O conquering Lord !
And the kingdom of Jesus on earth
    be restored. ·

Wave the Jubilee Flag over mountain and crag,
    For freedom and peace ;
And establish the reign which never shall cease !

All the heathen shall come unto Zion their home,
    And peoples and tongues,
United in Christ, break forth into songs.

Songs of triumph and mirth throughout the whole
    earth
    Shall Jesus restore ;
And nations shall never learn war any more.

None shall make them afraid ; every man undis-
    mayed
    Shall sit under his vine,
Rejoicing in Christ and favour Divine.

He will gather the meek, the halting and weak,
 And seal them His own,
And make in Mount Zion His permanent Throne.

There Jesus shall reign, and His kingdom maintain
 Till His foes are subdued ;
All pardoned, and sprinkled with covenant blood.

O Zion, arise ! and lift up thine eyes,
 Thy glory is near !
And soon shall thy day of salvation appear.

Haste, Jubilee day ! O ye clouds, pass away !
 Sun of Righteousness, rise !
O Jesus, come quickly ! descend from the skies !

By the power of Thy blood let mankind be
 renewed—
 Every heart Thine abode,
And flourish like Eden, the garden of God.

THE CLOUD OF WITNESSES.

" Wherefore seeing we also are compassed about with so great a cloud of witnesses, let us lay aside every weight, and the sin which doth so easily beset us, and let us run with patience the race that is set before us."—HEBREWS xii. 1.

HAT a bright and blissful band !
There before the Throne they stand ;
There receive a full reward,
In the presence of their Lord.

Clothed in robes of radiant white,
Crowned with gladness, filled with light,
Through Eternity they prove
Growing rapture, life, and love.

What are all their sufferings now ?
With a crown upon their brow,
Through their martyr-pangs they share
All the weight of glory there.

Vanquished now are Sin and Death ;
Conquered they through mighty faith ;
Through a sea of blood they came
To the New Jerusalem.

Prophets, Martyrs, Saints unite ;
There they stand in ranks of light ;
Golden harps and songs of joy
Evermore their tongues employ.

Jesu ! Saviour ! may we be
Faithful followers of Thee ;
Bear the Cross, in meekness bear,
Then the Crown of Victory wear.

WHAT MEANEST THOU, O SLEEPER?

"So the shipmaster came to him, and said unto him,
What meanest thou, O sleeper? arise, call upon thy God,
if so be that God will think upon us, that we perish not."
—JONAH i. 6.

WHAT meanest thou, O sleeper?
  God's anger frowning o'er thee,
Securely sleeping in Satan's
    keeping,
  With Death and Hell before thee !
O hear the voice of warning !
  Christ only can deliver ;
Open thine eyes, awake ! arise !
  Or thou art lost for ever !

The storm is darkly gathering ;
  See the red lightning's flashing !
God's righteous wrath athwart thy path
  Rolls like an earthquake crashing.
The surging waves roar near thee,
  Of death that dieth never ;
Start from thy sleep, nor madly leap
  The gulph that burns for ever.

The World, the Flesh, the Devil,
In league intend thy ruin,
And every breath leads on to death,
And works thy soul's undoing.
What meanest thou, O sleeper?
From sin and Satan sever;
To Jesus fly while mercy's nigh,
Or thou art lost for ever.

To sleep is sure destruction,
And fiery indignation;
Down in the lake of Hell to wake,
To endless condemnation.
What meanest thou, O sleeper?
To die without endeavour,
And sink to Hell in flames to dwell,
Amidst the lost for ever!

What meanest thou, O sleeper?
God give thee now a waking;
Let thunders roll over thy soul,
Thy soul in terror quaking!
O come to Christ for pardon,
From sin and Satan sever;
Wash in the flood of Jesu's blood,
And thou art saved for ever!

THE BATTLE CALL.

"Soldiers of Christ, arise,
  And put your armour on,
Strong in the strength which God supplies
  Through His eternal Son."

CHARLES WESLEY.

RISE, ye conquering legions,
    The trumpet-blast is sounding ;
  Ye men of might, go forth and fight,
    Your hearts with courage bounding :
King Jesus is your Captain,
  Omnipotent and glorious ;
His name is power, His arm a tower,
  His hosts are all victorious.

Up with the blood-stained banner,
  Your standard be unfurled ;
Follow your flag, o'er sea and crag,
  All round the ransomed world.
Shout for your Captain's glory ;
  Unsheathe your two-edged swords ;
Stand to your arms, through all alarms,
  The battle is the Lord's !

The Martyrs' noble army,
  In the same cause uniting,
Like Stephen stood, baptized in blood,
  And died for Jesus fighting.
They fell, but falling conquered,
  The world and sin defying ;
On earth they fell, in Heaven to swell
  Christ's victories by dying.

Then march your bright battalions,
  Fresh conquests still obtaining,
And blood-bought bands, in distant lands,
  For Jesu's subjects gaining.
From conquering to conquer,
  O'er every land and nation,
Go and proclaim King Jesu's name,
  The Captain of Salvation.

Smite the strongholds of Satan,
  The waning crescent shiver ;
Sweep idol-gods from their abodes,
  And every slave deliver :
Through the broad earth spread freedom
  Of body, soul, and spirit,—
Freedom in Christ, and joy unpriced,
  For all men to inherit.

Arise, ye conquering legions,
  Your Captain's word is spoken,
That " every knee shall bow to Me,"—
  Nor can His word be broken :

Haste the millennial glory,
  The conflict, then the crown ;
When war shall cease, and Heaven's own peace,
  The Prince of peace, come down.

ON THE DEATH OF A YOUNG LADY.

HE is gone to the land of the blest,
   From the region of sorrow and night ,
She hath snatched immortality's vest,
   And mantled her spirit in light :
By the throne-blaze of Godhead she stands,—
   The ministering Angels have crowned her,—
Eternity's harp in her hands,
   And a halo of glory around her.

She hath grappled and triumphed o'er Death,
   And passed through his caverns of gloom ;
She hath drawn the unquenchable breath
   That defies e'en the thunders of doom :
Outspread are her gossamer wings,
   O'er the azure of boundless repose ;
And she drinks of the nectar which springs
   Where the river of Paradise flows.

Then weep not, though thus she hath fled,
   In the blossom of beauty and prime ;
The flower is transplanted, not dead,
   The sunshine of Heaven is her clime.
'Twere cruel to pray for her back,
   Since her glorified soul is at rest ;
Then weep not, but follow her track,—
   She has gone to the land of the blest.

CHRISTIAN FIDELITY.

"Be thou faithful unto death, and I will give thee a crown
of life."—REVELATION ii. 10.

E thou faithful unto death ;
  Maintain the glorious strife ;
  Battle to thy latest breath,
   To win the Crown of Life :
Jesus holds the glittering prize,
  For all that to the end endure ;
Onward, upward, toward the skies,
  And victory is sure.

Strong thou art, in strength Divine,
  To conquer every foe ;
Earth and hell in vain combine
  To lay the Christian low.
In the heart where Jesus dwells,
  Sweetly with His presence blest,
Holy courage ever swells,
  And fills and fires the breast.

Be thou faithful unto death,
   Till every foe, subdued,
Falls before the power of faith,
   Triumphant through the Blood.
Onward, upward, heavenward still,
   O bear the cross, and urge the strife;
Thou shalt stand on Zion's hill,
   And wear the Crown of Life.

CHRIST IN THE SYNAGOGUE.

"And He was teaching in one of the synagogues on the Sabbath. And, behold, there was a woman which had a spirit of infirmity eighteen years, and was bowed together, and could in no wise lift up herself."—St. Luke xiii. 10, 11.

IN the Synagogue of old,
   On the Sabbath day, behold
      A lonely mourner kneeling;
      Meanly clad and poor was she,
   A woman in adversity,
      Her depth of sorrow feeling:
   But silent in unuttered woe
   Her bitter tears of anguish flow.

Crushed beneath her weight of grief,
Still she comes to find relief,
   Or strength for patient bearing:
O woman! trembling in thy tears,
By Satan bound for eighteen years,
   Cast down, and nigh despairing,
Bowed together without hope,
Bent, unable to look up!

Years of pain, all dark and dreary ;
Days and nights, alas ! how weary !
    Deepest suffering—keenest sorrow,
Inward agony of soul;
Under Satan's fierce control,
    Without one brightening morrow ;
Abraham's daughter she, but bound
By the fiend of hell around.

O sad woman ! in thy grief
God will send thee sure relief,
    And break thy bonds asunder :
Late deliverance comes at length ;
Youthful vigour, health, and strength,
    And peace, and joy, and wonder,
Mingle in thy sweet surprise,
Glow in rapture from thine eyes.

Jesus comes to set thee free;
Stronger than thy foe is He ;
    He heals the broken-hearted :
There thy great Deliverer stands,
Calls thee, and lays on His hands,
    And virtue is imparted.
By that touch, mind, body, soul,
In a moment are made whole.

Joyous woman ! all elate,
Like an Angel, now made straight,
    Upward, heavenward, look for ever !

Shout thy loving Saviour's praise,
Trust Him all thy lengthened days,
  Almighty to deliver!
Satan hath no power on thee;
God's own Son hath set thee free.

Trembling sinner! tied and bound,
Listen to the Gospel sound.
  Jesus calls *thee*, wilt thou come?
Prostrate, lowly at His feet,
Thou shalt sure deliverance meet;
  Pardon, freedom, refuge, home,
All in Jesus thine shall be,
When He lays His hands on thee.

THE REFUGE.

"And a man shall be as an hiding place from the wind, and a covert from the tempest."—ISAIAH xxxii. 2.

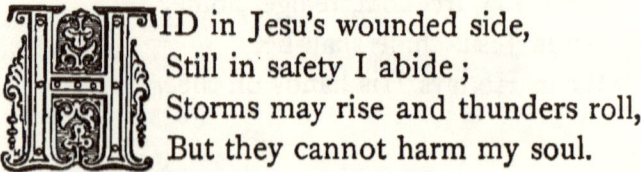ID in Jesu's wounded side,
Still in safety I abide;
Storms may rise and thunders roll,
But they cannot harm my soul.

Strong temptations may assail,
Stronger faith will yet prevail;
Sin and Satan are subdued
By the virtue of His blood.

Jesus is my living Head,
Jesus is my daily bread;
Me He for His " brother " owns,
Of His body, flesh and bones.

Hid in Jesu's wounded side,
I will evermore abide;·
Safe amid the tempest's strife,
Till I grasp the Crown of Life.

THE INVITATION.

"Ho, every one that thirsteth, come ye to the waters."
ISAIAH lv. 1.

HO, every one that thirsteth,
   Hear Jesu's invitation
Your thirst to slake! O come and take
   The waters of salvation!
All ye that have no money,
   Come to the flowing river,
For milk and wine, and bread Divine,
   And eat and live for ever.

Ye lame, and halt, and weary,
   O come to be relieved!
Jesus will grant whate'er ye want,
   And all shall be received.
Come to your loving Saviour,
   Who gives this gracious token,
To contrite hearts His love imparts,
   And gently heals the broken.

O seek for pardoning mercy,
   While mercy still is proffered!
While God is near, in humble fear
   Accept the pardon offered.

O cry for true repentance,
    The Spirit's mighty waking,
And turn to God, through Jesu's blood,
    Thy every sin forsaking !

Come to the open Fountain,
    For every sinner free ;
That blood was spilt to cleanse *thy* guilt,
    And now avails for thee.
Abundant pardon waits thee,
    Heaven's bliss lies straight before thee,
Good Angels yearn for thy return,
    To strike their harps in glory.

Come, then, O trembling sinner !
    Hear Jesu's invitation ;
Accept His love, and sweetly prove
    His promise of salvation.
Bid doubt and sorrow vanish,
    From sin and Satan sever ;
In Jesu's strength cry out at length,
    " I am the Lord's for ever ! "

THE TRIUMPHANT WARRIOR.

[WRITTEN ON THE DEATH OF AN AGED MINISTER.]

OLDIER of Christ, well done !
Thy fight of faith is won ;
Helmet, shield, and sword lay down :
Faithful veteran of thy Lord,
Rise and grasp thy high reward !
Drop thine armour ! take thy Crown !

Life's conflict now is o'er ;
Rest, rest for evermore,
    In Heaven's serene :
Deep tranquillity be thine,
Eternal and Divine,
    No storms between.

Calm was thy dying hour :
Death came, but had no power
    Thy soul to scare :
The valley blazed with light,
And Jordan's waves grew bright,
    For Christ was there.

What songs of triumph rose !
Hark ! o'er thy vanquished foes
   Hosannahs ring !
" Shout ! for I long to die :
Grave, where's thy victory ?
   Death, where's thy sting ?"

So dies the man of God :
His Father's staff and rod
   His succour prove ;
Placid as Summer's even,
His spirit soars to Heaven
   On wings of love.

Gird up thy loins like him,
That when life's fitful dream
   Of care and strife
In death's lone hour shall break,
Thy deathless soul may wake
   To endless life.

Soldier of Christ, well done !
Thy fight of faith is won ;
Helmet, sword, and shield lay down :
Faithful veteran of thy Lord,
   Rise and grasp thy high reward !
Drop thine armour ! take thy Crown !

THE HOUR OF DEATH.

"O death, where is thy sting? O grave, where is thy
victory."—1 CORINTHIANS xv. 55.

HUSH ! 'tis the hour of death !
 The Messenger is come ;
With silent step and bated breath
 Enter the dying-room.
An aged saint lies there ;
 Wouldst thou the conflict see,
 And hear the shout of victory,
 And learn the power of prayer,
 And watch the struggle nearly past,
 The fiercest battle, and the last?
Here, by the bedside kneeling down,
 While fiery darts fly thick and fast,
See how the Christian wins the Crown.

 Jesus the Lord is here,
 'Tis He forbids to fear ;
Else would the tremulous sufferer yield,
 By age and feebleness brought low :
How could she take the field,
And handle sword and shield,
 And conquer *such* a foe ?

But mighty prayer prevails,
    And weakness is made strong ;
And Satan cowers and quails,
And now no more assails,
    But vanquished flies,
While hymns of triumph rise,—
    The victor's song !

All triumph now and joy,
    All clear and bright ;
No shade of sin's alloy
    Dims her pure sight.
With quivering lip and broken voice,
She bids us " shout," and cries " rejoice ! "
    Waving her palsied hand,
    She sights the happy land,
And death is now a sweet release ;
    The conflict ends in peace.
She sleeps, the deathless spirit fled ;
    She sleeps, the saint is dead !
The struggle past, the victory won,
    The silver cord is riven ;
But the spirit is before the Throne,
    And glorified in Heaven.

FOR THE DEAD IN CHRIST.

" Blessed are the dead which die in the Lord from henceforth : Yea, saith the Spirit, that they may rest from their
labours; and their works do follow them."—REVELATION
xiv. 13.

LESSED are the dead, who die
    In Christ their glorious Lord ;
    They mount up beyond the sky,
    And gain their great reward :
Conquerors in the final hour,
    Their latest foe in death o'ercome ;
Safe beyond the tempter's power,
    In Heaven their happy Home.

They shall hunger now no more,
    Nor ever thirst again ;
All their sufferings are o'er,
    And all their grief and pain :
Now before the Throne they stand,
    Clothed in robes of purest white ;
Palms of victory in their hand,
    With all the saints in light.

Where the living waters flow,
   The Lamb shall gently lead ;
They shall higher raptures know,
   On heavenly manna feed.
God shall wipe away their tears ;
   Filled with bliss, their bliss prolong :
Each a crown of victory wears,
   And sings the victor's song.

Blessèd are the dead who die
   In Christ their glorious Lord ;
To the haven of rest they fly,
   Their Paradise restored.
Soon the Judgment-trump shall sound,
   And soul and body join again,
Radiant and immortal, crowned,
   With Christ to live and reign.

GLORIFIED MARTYRS.

"Let our full hearts be reminded, that from Britain's manly sons and gentle daughters and helpless children, has gone up the last triumphant battalion of the glorious army of Martyrs. Ours was the last shout of triumph in Heaven; and hands which have been folded in ours are grasping the newest branches of palm."—*Extract from a Sermon by* DEAN ALFORD, *preached in Canterbury Cathedral after the Indian Massacre, All Saints' Day,* 1857.

THE Martyr-army of our God,
    In ecstasy and song,
    Long have Heaven's golden pavement
        trod,
Safe in their rich and high abode,
    And brightest of the throng :
Christ's noblest witnesses they stood,
Resisting even unto blood.

Triumphant host ! for Christ they died,
    Because He died for them :
Stoned, sawn asunder, crucified,
Or wrapt in fire, yet death defied,
    And shouted in the flame !
Christ's Martyrs, quivering at the stake,
Felt it high bliss, for His dear sake.

But who are these, upborne on high,
  On Angels' wings of down ?
On India's scorching sands they lie,
But rise to immortality,
  To wear the martyr's crown !
A new battalion swells the throng
Of Martyr-saints, a thousand strong.

The Martyr dies to live again,
  On history's page to glow ;
A Christian cannot die in vain,
A Martyr's death is priceless gain
  Of triumph o'er the foe :
Where'er the blood-red seed is sown,
The Church's richest grain is grown.

Think of them who have passed away,
  A squadron for the skies ;
Old England's bravest sons were they,
And gentle ones, and grandsires grey,
  A Moloch sacrifice !
But cruel death, and nameless wrongs,
Are changed for victory and songs.

Christ's Martyr-army round His Throne
  A loftier chorus swells !
Hands lately folded in our own
Wave palms in bliss and joy unknown,
  And dwell where Jesus dwells.
A sigh for Martyrs who have died,
A shout for Martyrs glorified !

FOR GOOD FRIDAY.

"The Lord hath laid on Him the iniquity of us all."
ISAIAH liii. 6.

OCKED and buffeted in scorn,
Scourged and bleeding, faint and
worn,
See the suffering Son of God,
Trembling, bends beneath our load ;
See Him, sinner, weeping see
Jesus crucified for thee.

Meekly yielding to His foes,
Onward calmly still He goes,
On His brow the thorny crown ;
Crimson drops fall streaming down,—
Tears of blood, O sinner, see !
Jesus weeping blood for thee.

On the Cross uplifted high,
There He hangs to bleed and die ;
" Numbered with transgressors " there,
Hear His agonizing prayer :—
" O my God ! I cry to Thee,
Why hast *Thou* forsaken Me ?"

There, transfixed, thy Saviour see,
Groaning on the cursèd tree;
O what throbbing anguish burst
In that bitter cry, "I thirst!"
Yet they gave Him, in His thrall,
Only vinegar and gall.

By His side the dying thief
Prays in penitential grief;—
"Lord remember me," he cries.
Mercy hears, and Love replies,
"Thou this very day shalt be
Safe in Paradise with Me!"

There, amidst the multitude,
Mary, Jesu's mother, stood,
In unutterable woe,
Deep as mother's heart can know;
Pierced, she heard His dying groan:
"Woman," now "behold thy Son!"

Darkened into sudden night,
Lo! the sun withdraws his light;
Earthquakes shake, and thunders roar,
While the graves their dead restore;
And the Temple's veil is rent,
By a Hand omnipotent.

Jesus dies upon the tree ;
Men and Angels stop and see !
By that agony and blood
Is appeased the wrath of God.
Heaven is opened, mercy free,
Through the blood of Christ, for me !

AN EASTER CAROL.

"And the Angel answered and said unto the women,
Fear not ye: for I know that ye seek Jesus, which was crucified. He is not here: for He is risen, as He said. Come, see
the place where the Lord lay."—St. Matthew xxviii. 5, 6.

CHRIST is risen from the dead,
    Let earth and Heaven rejoice !
Men and Angels, join to spread
    His praise, with heart and voice :
Join in hallelujahs, join
    Rapturous songs with one accord ;
Hymn His attributes Divine,
    And worship Christ the Lord !

Victor ! rising from the grave,
    By Thy right hand of power,
Mighty art Thou now to save ;
    Earth's millions are Thy dower.
By the travail of Thy soul,
    Thou Thy love to man hast showed ;
Trampled death, and death's control,
    And conquered by Thy blood.

Kneeling at Thy sacred feet,
   We worship and adore ;
Joy and sorrow strangely meet,
   And mingle evermore.
Where the cruel nails and spear
   Pierced Thee, hanging on the tree,
There we read Thy love most dear,
   Thy scars of victory see.

Talking with Thee by the way,
   Our hearts in rapture burn ;
Gladden us again to-day,
   Return, O Christ, return.
Breathe upon Thy Church and me,
   And break and bless the bread Divine ;
All our longing hearts would be
   Renewed, and made like Thine.

Gathering round our glorious Lord,
   At Bethany we stand ;
Sweetly falls His parting word,
   And consecrating hand.
While He spake, from earth He soared
   Upward, in majestic flight,
Soon by Angel-hosts adored,
   And hidden from our sight.

Baffled are the dark designs
   Of hell and Satan now;
Victory's crimson wreath entwines
   Around His sacred brow :

H

God of God, and Light of Light,
Thee, omnipotent, we own,
Reigning in Thy royal right,
On Heaven's eternal throne.

JESUS CHRIST EVER THE SAME.

"Jesus Christ the same yesterday, and to-day, and for ever."
HEBREWS xiii. 8.

NEVER will my Lord forsake
 Those that put their trust in Him :
In His arms who refuge take,
 He will succour and redeem ;
Save them from temptation's blast ;
Lift them up to Heaven at last.

Safety, comfort, joy, and peace,
 Come to all who firmly rest
On His blood and righteousness ;
 All who are of Christ possest,
They have chosen the good part,
Christ is dwelling in their heart.

Daily they by faith shall prove
 Christ is precious to their soul ;
Leaning on the breast they love,
 He will all their griefs console ;
And on those who love Him most
He will breathe the Holy Ghost.

Washed, and sanctified, and sealed,
 Numbered with His own elect,
With His grace and glory filled,
 What their glowing hearts expect
He will give to all His own,
And exalt them to a throne.

CONFESSING CHRIST.

St. Matthew x. 32, 33.

ESUS, may I never be
Worldly, and ashamed of Thee ;
Evermore may I proclaim
Thee, and glory in Thy name ;
Subject of Thy saving grace,
Thee continually confess.

Boldly may I bear the cross,
Boldly join Thy hallowed cause,
Boldly scorn and suffering share,
Boldly love to Thee declare ;
Sprinkled with Thy precious blood,
Boldly own Thee Lord and God.

Fired with zeal and filled with love,
Faithful may I always prove ;
Pray and preach, and labour still
My high calling to fulfil ;
Following Thee in life and word,
Thee my Saviour and my Lord.

Daily, in communion sweet,
Thee, O Jesus ! may I meet ;
Daily strengthened by Thy might,
Daily walking in Thy light,
Until from Thy glorious Throne
Thou shalt me, Thy follower, own.

CHILDREN'S SABBATH SONG.

"And the children crying in the temple, and saying,
Hosanna to the Son of David."—St. Matthew xxi. 15.

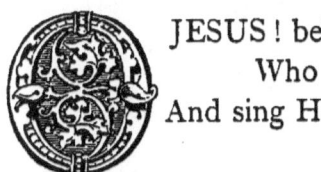 JESUS ! behold the lambs of Thy fold,
Who join in Thy praise,
And sing Hallelujah in rapturous lays.

Our loving hearts yearn for the Sabbath's return,—
Thine own holy day ;
And we hail with delight its earliest ray.

Every hour as it rolls brings peace to our souls,
And purest delight
In the service of Christ from morning till night.

In Thy Word we are told how children of old
By Jesus were blest,
Taken up in His arms and kindly caressed.

Hosanna they sang, and Jerusalem rang
With their beautiful songs :
Hosanna to Christ from thousands of tongues !

Like them we would join in worship Divine,
    And Jesus adore,
On earth and in Heaven, when time is no more.

Weak children are we, but trusting in Thee,
    And pleading Thy blood,
Through Jesus we find a reconciled God.

So we hail the bright day, more welcome than May,
    The best of the seven ;
And in worshipping Christ we anticipate Heaven.

When our Sabbaths are past and we get there at
    last,
    We'll sing of Thy grace,
And eternally bask in the smile of Thy Face.

THERE IS A LAND OF REST.

HERE is a land of rest,
    And undisturbed repose,
Where the pure river of the blest
    Through flowery pastures flows ;
Where all is joyous calm,
    And odorous perfume,
And the reposing victor's palm
    Is evermore in bloom.

No throbbing breast is there,
    Nor agonizing smart ;
No forehead wrinkled by despair,
    Nor madly aching heart ;
No lonely, long-drawn sighs,
    Nor sorrow's hopeless tears,
Rolling from dim and languid eyes,
    That wept for fourscore years.

No fierce and lawless flash
    Of young and headlong sin ;
No war-sword, with its reeking gash,
    Nor battle's horrid din ;

No death to snap the ties
  Of dear and holy love ;
No clouds o'ercurtaining the skies
  That smile in peace above.

Then let the tempest roar,
  And wreak its puny strife,
In Heaven the thunder rolls no more,
  The conflict ends with life :
Then gallantly each wild wave stem,
  Let courage man thy breast ;
There is a victor's diadem,
  There is a land of rest.

I AM GOING HOME TO GLORY.

I AM going home to glory,
    The land of light and love ;
Millions have gone before me,
    And are safely housed above,
In the mansions of the blessèd,
    Where sin and sorrow never come,
Prepared for me by Jesus,
    In my Father's house at Home.

The city lieth four-square,
    And its jasper walls are high ;
And twelve pearly gates are there,
    And twelve Angels standing by :
The broad and deep foundation
    Is of precious stones and gold ;
For ever bright, and always light,
    And glorious to behold.

No temple is therein,
    Nor need of sun or moon ;
For God's glory shineth ever,
    And brings eternal noon ;

And the nations of the savèd,
  In spotless robes of white,
With Christ the Lamb, and God, I AM,
  Walk evermore in light.

Beside the living fountains
  The Lamb doth gently lead,
And still unfold the bliss untold,
  And with heavenly manna feed :
No more sin, or grief, or sorrow
  Can ever enter there :
O land of light ! even now in sight,
  We long thy joy to share !

Amidst the burning sapphires,
  In triumph we shall stand,
And join, ere long, the rapturous throng,
  In yonder better land.
When every kingdom, every nation,
  Shall adore the great I AM,
And sing anthems of salvation
  To our God and to the Lamb.

THE LORD IS MY SHEPHERD.

PSALM xxiii.

HE Lord is my Shepherd, I never can
want,
In green living pastures He makes
me lie down,
And sweetly restores me when weary and faint ;
Beside the still waters He comforts His own,
And the sheep of His fold gathers up in His arms,
And calls them by name, and shields from alarms.

He leads me with gentle and loving constraint,
In paths which children of righteousness take,
And bends down His ear to my sorrowful plaint,
And pardons my sins for His own mercy's sake.
O the blessings which flow to the sheep of His
fold !
The Lord is my Shepherd, and no good He'll with-
hold.

Yea, though I walk through the valley of death,
Where the shadows are deep, and the spirit is
lone,
No fear will I feel, and no weakness of faith ;
For my Shepherd will ever take care of His own ;

He will comfort my soul with His staff and His
    rod,—
My Shepherd, the Shepherd of Israel, is God.

My table He spreads in the sight of my foes,
    And the oil of His grace anointeth my head ;
My Shepherd is mine, and my cup overflows,
    And my steps by goodness and mercy are led :
All the days of my life I will trust in His word,
And dwell evermore in the House of the Lord.

TO AN AFFLICTED FRIEND.

HOW gracious is our God,
Even though He use the rod !
Every stroke He gives to prove
To His child a father's love :
Never in vindictive wrath
Does He cross His children's path ;
When we hear our Father's call,
'Tis to save us from a fall.

When affliction lays us low,
And the waning pulse beats slow ;
When the tremulous hand grows weak,
And the tongue can hardly speak ;—
Then we learn, in sweet content,
Why affliction should be sent ;
Then, like children, we lie still,
Bear and bless our Father's will.

In the waters rough and deep,
Still our confidence we keep ;
Through the starless midnight drear,
All is well, for God is near.

If our Father but require,
We will triumph in the fire ;
Though the scorching flames enfold,
He will bring us forth as gold.

Firmly fixed on Christ the Rock,
What can our assurance shock ?
Though affliction try us here,
Courage, sufferer ! Heaven is near !
Low in calm submission lie,
Watching still thy Father's eye ;
Bear awhile the mortal strife,
Yonder is eternal life.

THE PRECIOUS BLOOD OF CHRIST.

" Who is this that cometh from Edom, with dyed garments
from Bozrah ? "—ISAIAH lxiii. 1.

THE blood, the precious blood,
  On Calvary shed for me !
O the blood, the precious blood,
  Which brings the sinner near to God,
And sets the captive free !
O the blood, the precious blood,
  From Jesu's wounded side !
See the blood, a crimson flood,
From His head, His hands, and feet !
Man's redemption is complete,
  The Son of God has died.
Through the blood, the precious blood,
  All may now be justified.

O the blood, the precious blood,
  On Calvary shed for me !
Now I cast my sinful load
On the all-atoning blood,
  And wait to be set free.
O the blood, the precious blood,
  This only is the sinner's plea !

I

Lyra Sabbatica.

Humbly now I pardon claim,
With the publican exclaim,
" God be merciful to me,"
Through the blood, the precious blood,
    The blood of Calvary!

O the blood, the precious blood,
    On Calvary shed for me !
Here I fix my hope and faith ;
This shall give me life in death,
    And songs of victory.
O the blood, the precious blood,
    On Calvary shed for me !
Yonder round the Throne on high,
From the countless multitude,
Over all the rest shall swell
This triumphant canticle :
O the blood, the precious blood,
    On Calvary shed for me !
O the blood, the precious blood,
Which brings the sinner near to God,
    And sets the captive free !

COME FROM THE FOUR WINDS.

"Come from the four winds, O breath, and breathe upon
these slain, that they may live."—Ezekiel xxxvii. 9.

COME from the four winds, O breath!
   And breathe upon these slain;
All the earth is full of death,
   And sin and sorrow reign.
Father, Son, and Holy Ghost,
   Hear the universal cry
Of Thy sacramental host,
   Who at Thy footstool lie.

Now in humble faith we plead
   The promise and the oath,
Waiting in this hour of need,
   Till Thou fulfil them both.
Honour now the precious Blood;
   O make good Thy royal word!
Send the Spirit like a flood,
   The Spirit of the Lord.

Never will we cease to pray,
   Till Thou thy Spirit give,
Turn our darkness into day,
   And cause the dead to live;

Till Thy glorious Church arise,
  And all the earth for Christ enfold,
Pure as Heaven's o'erarching skies,
  Or Paradise of old.

Never will we cease to pray,
  Till every sinful soul
Unto Jesus finds his way,
  And is by faith made whole.
Until all shall know the Lord,
  Still we cry, and cry again,—
Conquer with Thy Spirit's sword,
  And hasten Jesu's reign.

TO THE SOLDIERS OF CHRIST.

" That bloody banner see,
  And in your Captain's sight,
Fight the good fight of faith with me,
  My fellow-soldiers, fight!"

CHARLES WESLEY.

EN of Israel, rise and fight
    The battles of your Lord;
    Buckle on your armour bright,
    And grasp the Spirit's sword:
Lift the glorious banner high,
  And, following in your Captain's track,
Satan with a shout defy,
  And drive his legions back.

Hear the trumpet-blast resound,—
  To arms! to arms! it calls;
Upon such as are not found,
  The curse of Meroz falls:
Every soldier of the Cross,
  Join the ranks and take the field,
Counting earthly gain but loss,
  Till God's elect are sealed.

Tell the world that Jesus died,
   And lives to intercede;
ALL may feel the Blood applied,
   And be made free indeed:
ALL may claim the Spirit's power,
   To quicken and to save the lost;
This is the accepted time,
   Another Pentecost.

Men of Israel, rise and fight
   The battles of your Lord;
In the strength of Jesu's might,
   Proclaim the Gospel word.
To the crowded haunts of sin,
   O follow in your Captain's train!
Soon in triumph will begin
   His bright millennial reign.

FOR ALL SAINTS' DAY.

" I believe . . . . in the communion of Saints."
APOSTLES' CREED.

FOR all the Saints in Heaven and earth,
    One hallowed day is set apart
For deep communion, holy mirth,
    And mystic unity of heart :
One brotherhood of love unites,
    Which neither time nor death can sever ;
One song is sung, one joy delights
    The family of God for ever.

What shining ranks around God's throne !
    Confessors, martyrs, patriarchs, seers,
Gathered from every clime and zone,
    Since the world's infancy of years :
Blood-bought, and clothed in robes of white,
    Victors who sing the victor's song ;
For ever with the Saints in light,
    Their bliss ineffable prolong.

Earth's myriads join their songs to-day,
    And earth and Heaven in concert meet ;
O grand and universal lay !
    O heavenly song of songs complete !

Salvation, honour, glory, praise,
   From saints below and saints on high;
The hallelujah chorus raise
   To Christ through all eternity.

One throbbing heart, one burning love,
   Cements Christ's lovers to each other;
All have their common home above,
   And all in Christ an elder Brother:
And soon—no more to weep or roam,
   No wanderer lost—with palm and crown,
God's family shall meet at Home,
   And in their Father's House sit down.

TO THE SOUL.

THOU ethereal sun of being, soul,
  Best gift of God, and likest Him
  that gave,
Curbless and chainless trampler on
  control,
Victor o'er earth, and scorner of the grave,
Thou wert not made to be a tyrant's slave,
Nor yet the cringing parasite of kings,
Kissing the foot that spurns thee ; nor to crave
In common bondage earth's decaying things :
Fame is a schoolboy's dream ; gold cankers, and
  hath wings.

Soul ! *thou* wert made for freedom, life, and light ;
  For pleasures earth denies ; the vast and wild
Of intellectual bliss ; the calm and bright
  Of joy—Eternity's own child.
  Time cannot sate thee, though her gifts were piled
In one tall Babel-column to the skies ;
  The witchery of love hath vainly smiled
To bless thy panting hopes, and vainly rise
For thee the melting gush of Nature's harmonies.

For ever standing on the verge of Time,
    Plumed for the sunshine of unclouded spheres ;
Unmeet for tarriance here, and too sublime
    To change with every hue of mortal fears :
    Now rapt to gladness, or now drowned in tears,
Thy wing is ever soaring, and thine eye
    Pondering the flight of fastly rolling years ;
Impatient of the moments as they fly,
And gasping for thy birthright—immortality.

Suns shine to be extinguished ; all we see
    Or hear of Nature's glory shall expire ;
The marble, dented by the pilgrim's knee,
    The molten mountain with its womb of fire,—
    All, all shall sink before creation's Sire :
But still the soul, unharmed by ruin's plough,
    Unchanged amidst the desolator's ire,
Shall spring from the world's ashes with calm brow,
Hailing her God, and feel more deathless then
    than now.

TO A MINISTER OF CHRIST.

" Cry aloud, spare not, lift up thy voice like a trumpet, and show My people their transgression, and the house of Jacob their sins."—ISAIAH lviii. 1.

ESSENGER of love Divine,
    Highest dignity is thine ;
    Christ's ambassador thou art,
    Authorized by God, and sent
News of mercy to impart,
    Jesu's chosen instrument.
Publish still the royal grace,
    Wherever human feet have trod ;
Cry to all the ransomed race,
    " Be reconciled to God."

Still be valiant for thy Lord,
Still proclaim the saving word ;
    Warn, arouse, alarm, entreat :
Christ for every man hath died,
Bring the sinner to His feet,
    Gather round the Crucified :
Lift the glorious Cross on high,
Preach the sacrificial Blood,
Show the Ark of refuge nigh,
    Which rides above the flood.

Strong in Christ, be stronger still,
    Boldly do thy Master's will;
Storm the battlements of sin,
    Follow in the ancient track;
Conquer Satan, fight and win
    Earth from the invader back.
All the world to Christ belongs;
    Bow every knee to Jesus, bow,
Crown Him with exulting songs,
    The King of glory now.

Messenger of love Divine,
    Royal dignity is Thine;
Human weakness is made strong,
    Darkness flames with heavenly light;
On thy head the cloven tongue
    Beams in mystery and might:
Still repeat the Gospel call,
    And herald the Messiah's reign;
Until Satan's kingdom fall,
    And Jesus comes again.

RISE AND BUILD.

[FOR THE FOUNDATION OF A PLACE OF WORSHIP.]

ISE and build a house for God,
   Bring your free-will offerings now ;
On Mount Zion, His abode,
   Bow, in thankful homage, bow ;
Bring the silver and the gold,
   Let the streaming incense rise ;
Poor and rich, and young and old,
   Join in loving sacrifice.

Build a temple to His praise,
   Offer unto God His own ;
Songs of holy triumph raise,
   Lay with shouts the corner-stone ;
Dig the strong foundation deep,
   Turn in faith the yielding sod ;
Hearts and hands united keep,
   Work in love who work for God.

Pour the voice of mighty prayer,
   Heaven will come to your relief ;
Cast on God your every care,
   Stagger not through unbelief :

Daily labour, watch, and pray,
  Soon the top-stone shall appear ;
Multitudes keep holy day,
  Kneel, and wait, and worship here.

Hallelujah to the Lord !
  Now we join the heavenly host,
Now we laud with one accord,
  Father, Son, and Holy Ghost.
Holy Trinity, descend !
  Claim this temple for thine own ;
Keep and evermore defend,
  Make our humbled hearts Thy throne.

Here, as at Jerusalem,
  Let the fire of God come down ;
Send the consecrating flame,
  Every faithful message crown :
Conquering Jesus ! O appear,
  Gather thousands by Thy grace ;
Carry on Thy conquests here,
  Clasp the world in Thy embrace.

TO DIE IS GAIN.

[THE DEATH-BED EXPERIENCE OF AN EMINENT
CHRISTIAN, LATELY DECEASED.]

ALMLY trusting in the Lord,
   Submissive to His will,
   Resting on His faithful word,
     My strength is to sit still ;
Body, spirit, soul resigned,
   And sweetly passive at His feet,
Wait, till Jesu's loving mind
   Within me is complete.

Lingering on the border land,
   By Jordan's swelling tide,
Bold I grasp the hand Divine,
   And firm in faith abide ;
Quiet is my childlike heart,
   And weaned, though earthly ties be riven ;
Never will my Lord depart,
   But take me home to Heaven.

Though the outward man decay,
   The inner man is strong,—
Strong in Jesus, day by day,
   And glad in heart and tongue.

If I live 'tis Christ to live,
  And more of His dear love obtain ;
If the summons I receive
  To die, "to die is gain."

Should the enemy appear,
  To fill with fear or doubt,
Jesus, help me ! be Thou near,
  To cast the tempter out.
Arm my soul with faith Divine,
  And if temptation, like a flood,
Should assail me, be it mine
  To conquer through the Blood.

Finish, Lord, Thy work of grace,
  Though in affliction's fire ;
Let me see Thy cloudless Face,
  And then in peace expire.
Purified from every sin,
  O fit me for my heavenly Home :
Jesus ! come and dwell within,
  O Jesus, quickly come !

Faith with eagle glance descries
  The glorious land of light ;
Spreads her pinions for the skies,
  And longs to take her flight :
Upward, heavenward, Christward still,
  Soaring on the wings of love ;
Guided by my Father's will,
  To Paradise above.

Calmly trusting in the Lord,
  And filled with joy and peace,
I His faithfulness record,
  His truth and righteousness ;
With my latest breath proclaim,
  Christ can to the utmost save ;
Conqueror through His blood I am,
  And victor o'er the grave.

WILD FLOWERS.

"Consider the lilies of the field, how they grow."
ST. MATTHEW vi. 28.

GOD might have made this beauteous
earth,
And left it void of flowers;
No song-birds with their welcome
mirth,
No fragrant Summer bowers:
With nought to meet the eye or ear,
In sight or sound, but what was drear.

But all God's gifts are bountiful,
In providence and grace;
Only our laggard hearts are dull,
And love so slow of pace
To lay our offerings at His feet,
And praise His name with ardour meet.

Come forth! God's wild-flowers are in bloom
On every hand to-day:
The Hawthorn white, and yellow Broom,
And Honeysuckle gay;

And flowers of variegated hue,
All beautiful, await your view.

Wild flowers ! wild flowers ! go where you will,
    In green and quiet lane,
Or wood, or field, you meet them still,
    On mountain side or plain.
God's flowers are they ; no human hand
E'er planted one throughout the land.

The Cowslip blossoms in the field,
    The Violet in the hedge ;
And Lilies white the valleys yield,
    And blooming Water-sedge ;
And Hyacinth and Primrose join,
And Daisies are a gift Divine.

Stop at this rural little nook ;
    The wild Rose overhead
Hangs in festoons ; but closer look,
    The Pimpernel so red,
And Strawberry, choose this sunny spot,
And love's own pledge, " Forget me not."

Ten thousand times ten thousand flowers
    God plants and waters too ;
And sends us sunshine and soft showers,
    And southern breeze, and dew,
For children's joy and manhood's love,
To draw our hearts to Heaven above.

God gives their colours and their scent ;
The tiniest flower that blooms
Was formed by power omnipotent :
God mingles their perfumes ;
And Solomon, in pomp and ease,
Was not arrayed like one of these.

Gather God's wild flowers in their prime,
Which beautify the earth ;
Go forth with shouts at Summer time,
Sweet children, in your mirth :
·God's smile is in them, and they prove
The God of power is God of love.

TO MARY ON HER TWENTY-FIRST
BIRTHDAY.

HAT can I wish thee, Mary,
    Of all in Heaven or earth,
. From   the   upper or the nether
    springs
Whence blessings have their birth?
May thy guide be still the hand Divine, ·
And thy joys be daily new,
And peace and happiness be thine,—
Sweet peace, thy journey through.

Look back, one glow of mercy
    Lights up the pathway trod,
And every ray shoots upward,
    And points to Heaven and God.
On your cradle shone the Christmas light,
    From Bethlehem's star-lit plains,
And to-day the evergreen is bright,
    And the star of hope remains.

Look inward, keep thy peaceful heart
    Still calm in hopeful trust ;
The Master saith, " Abide in Me,"—
    Faithful He is, and just.

A loving heart can ne'er go wrong,
    That leans on Jesu's breast ;
And simple faith is ever strong,
    And sings itself to rest.

Look forward, love and hope inspiring
    The future with their hue,
High deeds of holy enterprise,
    And pleasures pure and new ;
A Martha in devotion meet,
    To Jesus mayst thou prove,
And, sitting at the Master's feet,
    A Mary in thy love.

Look upward ! clear and beautiful
    Are the azure skies above thee,
And Heaven is bright in crystal light,
    Encircling those that love thee :
The Land of Promise is in sight,
    From Pisgah's mountain see ;
Look upward ! fight the Christian fight,
    Its glories are for thee.

What can I wish thee, Mary,
    On this thy natal day ?
To choose with heart the better part,
    Which cannot pass away :
Then rest and peace shall still increase,
    Till thy last step be trod ;
And thy spirit springs on Angel's wings,
    To glory, Heaven, and God.

FUGITIVE THOUGHTS.

I.—LIFE.

IFE is a thing of shadowy dreams ; Eternity
The waking up into realities.
And what, O man, miscalculating man !
What is the substance of thy three-
score years,
Or threescore years and ten, if thou wilt have them,
When cast into the mighty scale, whose beam
Is everlasting being?

II.—DEATH.

An unseen, cold, and uninvited visitor,
Who hustles by the porter at the gate,
And the loquacious lackey at the door,
Although it be a palace ; rushes up,
Unceremonious, to the inner chamber ;
Giveth no card of entrance, doth not knock
Before he enters, though a king be there ;
Undraws the curtain of the princely couch,
And tips his arrows in the very room
Where monarchs breathe their last.

III.—THE GRAVE.

The grave is but the cold and narrow hall
In which we wait the resurrection morn ;
And he that wins eternity of joy,
Although a past eternity of waiting
May intervene, will be a glorious gainer.

IV.—RELIGION.

Wouldst thou be happy? Serve and love thy God ;
The soul is ever vacant till He comes
And makes therein His dwelling ; then it stands
On the world's brink, enwrapt in contemplation,
Still pondering on futurity and Heaven,
Until at length, expanding in its size,
It comprehends infinity, and swells
Into immortal and immense desires,
Gigantic as eternity, then flies,
Its sunshine Godhead, and its home the skies.

O FOR THE WINGS OF YONDER DOVE.

"And I said, O that I had wings like a dove! for then would I fly away, and be at rest."—PSALM lv. 6.

FOR the wings of yonder dove,
   That hovers o'er her nest !
Soon would I soar to worlds above,
   And be for aye at rest :
No mortal tie should hold me back ;
   I'd spurn earth's crumbling sod,
And speed along the glorious track
   That leads to Heaven and God.

Away ! away ! ere early dawn
   Had lit the torch of day,
My buoyant pinions should be gone
   Far on their upward way ;
By rolling clouds, and dazzling stars,
   And orbs of sunny light,
And comets with their blazing cars,
   For ever on their flight.

On ! on ! like lightnings would I fly,
  Up towards the heavenly Throne,
Where glory's visions never die,
  And death is overthrown.
O for the wings of yonder dove,
  That hovers o'er her nest !
Soon would I soar to worlds above,
  And be for aye at rest.

TO A STREAMLET.

BEAUTIFUL silvery wanderer,
   Who windest thy sweet way
Through flowery meads, still warbling
   A soft and quiet lay ;
By the shadowy wood, tall waving
   Its green ancestral plumes,
And the hedgerow, where the daisy
   Gives out its mild perfumes ;

Adown the sloping hill,
   And along the valley-deeps,
Laving one side of the Abbey wall,
   Where the mantling ivy creeps ;
Through the broad park of the rich,
   By the Castle's oaken door,
And chanting the same placid tune
   By the cottage of the poor ;—

Beautiful silvery wanderer,
   For ever fresh and free,
Why dost thou seek the river ?
   The river seeks the sea :

Sweet streamlet, wouldst not rather
  In thy rural home abide,
Than rush to the Atlantic,
  And foam with ocean's tide ?

Beautiful wanderer ! go not :
  The flowers that fringe thy way
Would surely droop and wither,
  And the tender grass decay ;
The bending willows love thee,
  And the wild-winged birds would pine ;
Beautiful streamlet, go not
  From this quiet home of thine.

COMMON FLOWERS.

"The flowers appear on the earth; the time of the singing of
birds is come."—SOLOMON'S SONG ii. 12.

ET them boast as they will of the flowers
   Which are grown by the noble and
      great,
I will sing of the cottager's bowers,
   And the gardens of lowly estate.
The commonest flower that we see
   Has a beauty and charm all its own ;
And the Violet scent is as free
   To the poor, as the Queen on the throne.

How sweet, when the Snowdrops appear
   In clumps, at the dawning of Spring ;
And the Crocus and Daffodil cheer
   Every heart with the promise they bring !
When the Primrose in clusters is seen,
   And the breeze wafts its welcome perfume ;
The sunnyward hedgerow is green,
   And the Cherry tree bursts into bloom !

What a chorus of birds all in song !
   How melting the nightingale's lay !
And the peasant hies whistling along, ·
   Enjoying the beauties of May.

His garden, now radiant with flowers,
  With Cowslips and Daisies is drest ;
And Lilacs bend down with the showers,
  Giving out their rich scents as they're prest.

And the chief of all beauties, the Rose,
  White, red, and mingled in hue,
The old-fashioned Rose, he still grows,
  The same as his grandfather grew :
The " bower," and the " moss "—there they smile,
  The joy and the pride of the poor;
Just over the low rustic stile,
  Or trained at the side of the door.

Then on Sundays, when Church-going bells
  So plaintively float on the air,
In the cottage what happiness dwells,
  When both father and mother are there !
The children, all dressed in their best,
  How they love the Spring flowers of our land !
Each takes one to Church in his vest,
  And "baby" holds one in his hand.

Let them boast, then, as much as they please,
  Of the flowers grown by noble and great ;
I will sing, 'mid the humming of bees,
  Of the gardens of humble estate.
God sends flowers for the rich and the poor ;
  But the commonest flower that is known
Is as sweet, and its colours as pure,
  To the poor, as the Queen on the throne.

TO AN ATHEIST.

"The fool hath said in his heart, There is no God."
PSALM xiv. I.

INSOLENT atom ! basking in the blaze
    Of sunshine, to be blasted by its light !
Peering with bold and misbelieving gaze,
    To probe the secrets of the Infinite.
Bow to thy God, or else the endless night
Of unillumined darkness will be thine.
    Canst *thou* o'ermatch Omnipotence ? or fight
With war of words against the arm Divine ?
Drop thy vain weaponry, and kneel a suppliant at
    His shrine !

O canst thou doubt, and look upon the sun,
    And pensive moon, and starry dome on high ;
Hear the loud tempest, see the ocean run,
    And mountains bending upward to the sky,
    And every season's sweet variety,—
The grass-blade, and the monarch oak, the birds
    Of joyous minstrelsy and rainbow dye,
The lion of the forest, and the herds
That bow in worship mute, and praise in all but
    words ?

Dallier with thunderbolts, amid the shafts
   Of thickening vengeance thou hast guiltier been
Than fallen Angels, with their many crafts
   Of long corroded and remorseless sin :
   They tremble ! but thou hast no dread within
The deep recesses of thy spirit's cell,
   That harbours the wild phantom-hope to win
The conflict—ringing thus thy own death-knell !
God tries on earth, rewards in Heaven, but punishes
   in hell.

Thou, of all beings on the peopled earth,
   Art the most wretched and deserted thing.
Soul without God ! it is a deathless birth
   Of misery and woe—destruction's wing
   Already darkens o'er thee ; and thy Spring
Of natural life shall wither without bloom,
   Summer without her fruits, and Autumn bring
The barren Winter of eternal gloom,
If, hapless wretch, thou wilt thus rush upon thy
   doom.

CHRIST A KING.

"My heart is inditing a good matter : I speak of the things
which I have made touching the King."—PSALM xlv. I.

Y heart is inditing a song
        To Jesus, my crown and my joy;
    My innermost soul and my tongue
        Delight in the hallowed employ.
I speak of the things I have made,—
My soul is on fire with pure love,—
To the King in His glory displayed,
Enthroned in His kingdom above.

O fairest of all that is fair !
O brightest of all that is bright !
Majestic in meekness to bear,
    And pure as the crystalline light :
Thy beauties of holiness shine,
    A halo all else to eclipse ;
The blaze of effulgence Divine,
    And grace, is poured into Thy lips.

O Jesus ! ride on in Thy might,
    Thy royal dominion proclaim ;
Let nations bow down and unite
    Their anthems of praise to Thy name :

L

By the sword of Thy Spirit subdue
  Earth's millions, her thrones and her kings ;
Thy right hand, in power ever new,
  Shall teach Thee terrible things.

How sharp are thine arrows of war,
  When thine enemies fall at thy feet,
Heart-stricken, with many a scar,
  And humbled in penitence meet !
But how mild and gentle Thy sway
  O'er such as submit to Thy reign !
Their sins are all taken away,
  And the wounded are eased of their pain.

Set up, O Immanuel ! Thy throne,
  Almighty on earth as in Heaven,
And gather mankind for Thine own,
  Redeemed by Thy blood, and forgiven.
The tribes of the heathen are Thine ;
  Revisit Thy purchase of old ;
Embrace them in mercy Divine,
  And bring in the world to Thy fold.

O come to Thy desolate Bride,
  And lift up her languishing head ;
In triumph millennial abide,
  Thy Church and her conquests to spread :
Most sweet are Thy garments with myrrh,
  And aloes and cassia blend ;
Thy coming no longer delay,
  O Jesus ! in glory descend.

CHRIST A PRIEST.

"The Lord hath sworn, and will not repent, Thou art a Priest for ever after the order of Melchizedek."—PSALM cx. 4.

OUT of Zion God shall send
　　The rod of Jesu's strength ;
All His enemies shall bend
　　And bow to Him at length :
He shall make His raging foes,
　　Subdued beneath His footstool, cower ;
His millennial reign disclose,
　　His kingdom come with power.

God's anointed One is He,
　　With sacred unction crowned ;
Now His travail shall He see,
　　And now His joy abound :
Willing millions bow to Him,—
　　Him, bright in holiness and truth ;
Radiant as the morning's beam,
　　In all the dew of youth.

God, the mighty God, hath sworn,
　　And never will repent ;
Jesus, who our sin hath borne,
　　By God the Father sent ;

God in man, and man in God,
   Humbled lower than the least,—
" Thou, who hast the winepress trod,
   Art evermore a Priest."

Evermore Thy precious Blood,
   O Lamb of God ! shall plead ;
Earth, with righteousness o'erflowed,
   Thy glorious toil succeed :
Willing, in Thy day of power,
   Bow every heart and every knee ;—
Come in this accepted hour,
   And set Thy people free.

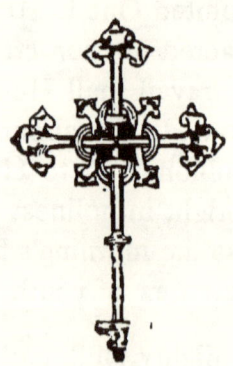

FOR THE PROMISED SPIRIT.

" And I believe in the Holy Ghost, the Lord and giver of
life."—NICENE CREED.

COME, ye who desire an answer by fire,
    And long for the day
  When Jesus His sceptre o'er all
    men shall sway,

Join the catholic cry for the power from on high,
    The Spirit Divine,
And pray till you get the life-giving sign.

With importunate prayer your petitions declare,
    And mightily cry,
Expecting just now a gracious reply.

Through the covenant Blood which on Calvary
    flowed,
    The Spirit is ours ;
And the blessing is promised in plentiful showers.

For the Spirit we pray ; no longer delay,
    O Fire from on high !
Descend, Lord and giver of life, while we cry !

In shaking and might, in glory and light,
    On every brow,
Thou Spirit of burning, come, visit us now.

Every heart cries, "Come in, and cleanse me from
    sin
        In Jesus's blood ;
And fill with the Spirit and glory of God."

O let the heavens rend ! Holy Spirit, descend
    In Pentecost power,
Till the heathen are gathered to Christ as His
    dower.

O Jesus ! all hail ! let Thy Gospel prevail,
    Till the world is o'erspread,
And Paradise blooms with life from the dead.

THE COMING MILLENNIUM.

"Awake, awake; put on thy strength, O Zion; put on thy beautiful garments, O Jerusalem, the holy city: for henceforth there shall no more come into thee the uncircumcised and the unclean."—ISAIAH lii. 1.

WAKE! awake! O Zion!
Put on thy strength Divine,—
Thy garments, bright in beauty,—
The Bridal dress be thine:
Jerusalem the holy,
To purity restored;
Meek Bride, all fair and lowly,
Go forth to meet thy Lord.

From henceforth pure and spotless,
All glorious within,
Prepared to meet the Bridegroom,
And cleansed from every sin;
With love and wonder smitten,
And bowed in guileless shame,
Upon thy heart be written
The new mysterious name.

Jerusalem the holy,
In light and peace behold;
Her glowing altars flaming,
Her candlesticks of gold.

The heavenly Bridegroom's dwelling,
　The place of David's thrones;
Her solemn anthems swelling,
　Her pavement precious stones.

Jerusalem, victorious
　In triumph o'er her foes;
Mount Zion, great and glorious,
　Thy gates no more shall close:
Earth's millions shall assemble
　Around thine open door,
While hell and Satan tremble,
　And earth and Heaven adore.

The Lamb who bore our sorrows
　Comes down to earth again;
No sufferer now, but Victor,
　For evermore to reign;
To reign in every nation,
　And rule in every zone:
O world-wide coronation!
　In every heart a throne.

Awake! awake! O Zion!
　Thy Bridal Day draws nigh,—
The day of signs and wonders,
　And marvels from on high:
Thy sun uprises slowly,
　But keep thou watch and ward;
Fair Bride, all pure and lowly,
　Go forth to meet thy Lord.

FOR THE CONVERSION OF ENGLAND.

FATHER, Son, and Holy Ghost,
   Hear Thy suppliant Church's cry ;
See Thy Eucharistic host
   Low in Lenten sackcloth lie,
Waiting, weeping at Thy feet,
   One in heart, of one accord,—
O send down the Paraclete !
   O fulfil Thy faithful word !
Every head with glory crown,
Holy Ghost, come down, come down !

On the Queen upon her throne,
   On the noble and the great,
Unto such as dwell alone,
   Coldly in their high estate ;
Where the merchant princes stand,
   All too prone to worship gold,
Where the thoughtless myriad band,
   Tied and bound in Satan's hold,—
Bare Thine arm ! the heavens rend !
Holy Ghost, descend, descend !

Where the thousands congregate,
  Under the Cathedral dome,
Or in solemn Minster wait,
  Sin-convincing Spirit, come!
Where the Gospel trumpet sounds,
  Visit every house of prayer;
Where iniquity abounds,
  Grace.abounding triumph there !
Jesus ! let Thy power be shown,
Gather England for Thine own.

Father, Son, and Holy Ghost,
  Hear Thy suppliant Church's cry ;
Help Thy blood-besprinkled host;
  Out of Zion strength supply ;
Give the mighty power of prayer,
  Faith, and unity, and love ;
Suddenly, O Christ, appear !
  Until *all* Thy mercy prove :
England's Pentecostal crown,
Holy Ghost, come down, come down !

FOR THE CONVERSION OF THE WORLD.

" For every battle of the warrior is with confused noise, and garments rolled in blood; but this shall be with burning and fuel of fire."—ISAIAH ix. 5.

PLIFT the blood-red banner,
 Unsheath the Spirit's sword;
Put on the Christian's armour,
 The armour of the Lord ;
The helmet of salvation,
 And faith's victorious shield;
Go forth with acclamation,
 The world your battle-field.

Every battle of the warrior,
 Who fights by land or flood,
Is with confusèd noise,
 And garments rolled in blood ;
But this shall be with burning,
 From Heaven its light shall shine,
God's Spirit overturning,—
 The fire of love Divine.

Uplift the blood-red banner,
 And shout, with trumpet's sound,
Deliverance to the captive,
 And freedom to the bound ;

Earth's jubilee of glory,
  The year of full release :
O tell the wondrous story;
  Go forth and publish peace !

Go forth, confessors, martyrs,
  With zeal and love unpriced,
And preach the blood of sprinkling,
  And live or die for Christ :
For Christ claim every nation,
  Your banner wide unfurled;
Go forth and preach salvation,
  Salvation for the world !

GIVE THE KING THY JUDGMENTS.

PSALM lxxii.

GIVE the King Thy judgments, Lord,
    Thy righteousness display;
    Jesus ! wield Thy conquering sword,
    Assert Thy royal sway:
Over Heaven, and earth, and hell,
    Reign in majesty supreme ;
Come again in peace to dwell
    With those Thou didst redeem.

Come and break th' oppressor's chain,
    And bid the slave go free ;
O send down the gentle rain
    On all mankind and me:
Light of life ! Thy radiance shed
    From sea to sea, from shore to shore ;
Thy imperial glory spread,
    Till time shall be no more.

Clothe Thine enemies with shame,
    And wear Thy regal crown;
At the mention of Thy name
    Let earthly kings bow down ;

Every nation, clime, and tongue,
  Kneel in homage at Thy feet;
Earth, in universal song,
  Our Jesu's praise repeat.

Live and reign, O glorious King!
  In every heart and home;
Peace and joy and gladness bring;
  O Jesus, quickly come!
Gather in the needy poor,
  And save the souls of all mankind;
Open wide the Gospel door,
  That all may mercy find.

On the arid mountain-top
  Let waving corn appear;
And the Gospel manna drop
  On deserts parched and drear.
O ye cities of the earth,
  Flourish as the fruitful field;
Jubilant with hallowed mirth,
  All sanctified and sealed.

Live for ever, glorious King,
  Thy name for aye endure;
Let the Church her anthems sing,
  For victory is sure.
Blessèd be the Lord our God,
  And blessèd be His glorious name;
Be His glory spread abroad,
  Through earth and Heaven the same.

CHILDREN'S MISSIONARY HYMN.

OME, children, and join, with ardour
Divine,
And help to do good,
By publishing peace through Jesus's
blood.

The heathen abroad are longing for God,
And looking to you ;
Let them see what the children in England can do.

The Jesus you love, who came from above,
Your souls to redeem,
Died that heathen and Negroes might come unto
Him.

But on millions redeemed no light ever beamed,
And Christ is unknown ;
For the Jubilee trumpet has never been blown.

O send the glad news to Gentiles and Jews ;
The Gospel proclaim ;
And world-wide salvation, in Jesus's name.

Come, children, and sing, to Jesus our King,
     Hallelujahs of joy,
Such as Angels and glorified spirits employ.

Come, children, and pray, " Lord, hasten the day
     When the earth shall be filled
With glory, and Christ in His kingdom revealed !"

Come, children, and give, and Christ will receive
     Whatever is given ;
And your offerings arise, like sweet incense, to
    Heaven.

Come, children, and join, with ardour Divine,
     And sanctified mirth ;
Sound the Jubilee blast to the ends of the earth.

THE CHURCH'S SECURITY.

" Great is the Lord, and greatly to be praised in the city of our God, in the mountain of His holiness."—PSALM xlviii. 1.

GREAT is the Lord our God :
  In Zion His abode,
  In the mountain of His power,
    There in solemn state He reigns ;
  There, a refuge and a tower,
  He His holy Church maintains.

Mount Zion, His delight,
  How beautiful and bright !
  Mark ye well her bulwarks strong,
    See her palaces arise,
  Sanctified by prayer and song,
  In communion with the skies.

There Israel's God is known,
  And loves and guards His own ;
  'Stablishes His Church on earth,
    In the bonds of heavenly love :
  Sweetly joined, in mystic mirth,
  With the glorious Church above.

M

O dear and joyous rest,
With Jesu's presence blest ;
There the Gospel feast is spread,
　　Richer far than Angels' food,—
Jesu's flesh, the living bread,
　　Jesu's sacramental blood.

There harmony and love
Ineffable we prove ;
Father, Son, and Holy Ghost,
　　Pardons, sanctifies, and seals ;
While, in growing raptures lost,
　　Jesus His new Name reveals.

O Zion ! lift Thy voice ;
Triumphantly rejoice :
God is in the midst of thee ;
　　Walls of fire are thy defence :
Rest secure, from danger free,
　　Circled by Omnipotence.

Sheltered in Jesu's side,
God is our strength and guide ;
Washed in Christ's atoning blood,
　　Earth and hell in vain unite :
All our foes shall be subdued,
　　We shall join the saints in light.

CHRISTMAS SONNETS.

I.—THE STAR.

"When they saw the star, they rejoiced with exceeding great joy."—ST. MATTHEW ii. 10.

STAR of stars! most luminously bright,
    And beaming forth in lustre all thine own,
    Like a fair diamond on the brow of night,
A traveller thou from some celestial zone,
    On thy first visit to a sphere unknown,—
Whence comest thou, O clear and brilliant star,
    Moving in silent majesty along
The dark expanse to Bethlehem afar,
    To shine in glory there, and there prolong
Thy stay, till earth and Heaven unite in song?
O star of stars! sweet, radiant, welcome stranger,
    God's light art thou, to guide the weary feet
Of the wise men to yonder lowly manger,
    Where, on His mother's breast, the Infant God they greet.

II.—THE ANGELS.

" And suddenly there was with the Angel a multitude of the heavenly host praising God, and saying, Glory to God in the highest, and on earth peace, good-will toward men."—ST. LUKE ii. 13, 14.

HUSHED in the silence of night's deep repose,
　　The shepherds watched their flocks, and all was still,
Save the low, melancholy bleat, which rose
　　At intervals, and echoed o'er the hill,
　　Where midnight's breezy breath grew bleak and chill.

There sat the shepherds in calm rumination,
　　When sudden glory lit both earth and sky;
Around them shone Heaven's bright illumination;
　　And a winged Angel, robed in light, stood by,
　　Proclaiming Christ the Lord, and peace brought nigh.

Then came Heaven's choristers, a glittering throng
　　Of Angels, singing as they sing above,—
Full-voiced, and joining in triumphant song
　　Of Jesu's blessèd birth, and peace, and heavenly love.

III.—THE SHEPHERDS.

"And there were in the same country, shepherds abiding in the field, keeping watch over their flock by night."— ST. LUKE ii. 8.

THRILLED with the heavenly anthems they had heard,
　　And the glad tidings of a Saviour's birth,
Not long the shepherds lingered, deeply stirred

By the high psalmody of Angel-mirth,
And God's own message of good-will to earth.
Ere the stars paled before the dawning day,
  With growing wonderment, and mingled awe,
Towards Bethlehem they bent their silent way,
  And there, with reverent gaze, their Lord they saw
Cradled with oxen, on a bed of straw.
Then sang the shepherds of the wondrous Child,
  And made the Angel's visit known abroad;
And holy hymns their homeward way beguiled,
  While their full hearts rejoiced, in love and praise
    to God.

IV.—THE SAVIOUR.

" Unto you is born this day in the city of David a Saviour,
  which is Christ the Lord."—ST. LUKE ii. 11.

OPEN the door, and in a manger see
  God manifest below! The Infant there,
Smiling in weakness on His mother's knee,
  Is God's eternal Son, whose shoulders bear
The government of earth, and sea, and air:
Hell trembles at His presence and His power;
  But, stooping from His royalty supreme,
He comes to seek and save, and blessings shower
  On rebel man, in one eternal stream:
  He comes to conquer, and by blood redeem:
His arm shall crush His foes; His sceptre sway
  Omnipotent, while men and Angels bow.
O Babe! that once in Mary's bosom lay,
  Come to Thy ransomed world, and claim Thy
    Kingdom now.

CHRISTMAS CAROLS.

No. I.

(FOR CHILDREN.)

COME, children, and raise a choral of
        praise
            To Jesus your King,
    Who came down from Heaven salva-
    tion to bring.

O hasten with me, and at Bethlehem see
        The wonderful Child,—
The beautiful Babe, by sin undefiled.

Let us follow the star, which shines from afar,
        O'er the place of His birth,
And join with the Angels in anthems of mirth.

O how sweet is the song ! of the glorified throng
        How welcome the strain
Of glory to God, and good-will unto men !

O how blessèd the news to Gentiles and Jews,
        No longer forlorn !
In the city of David a Saviour is born !

Standing over the place, to publish the grace,
    Star of Bethlehem, shine !
A gem for the crown of the Infant Divine.

The shepherds are there, His praise to declare,
    And return on the road
To their homes, singing praise and glory to God.

The wise men behold, with offerings of gold,
    In reverence meet,
Lay their gifts of frankincense and myrrh at His
feet.

There, humble and lone, uncared for, unknown,
    With the ox in his stall,
Lies the Infant of days, the Monarch of all.

O Jesus, we bow and worship Thee now,
    Our Saviour and Friend !
Embrace in Thine arms, and keep to the end.

In the manger reclined, Messiah we find,—
    O humble abode,
To shelter the Only Begotten of God !

O children rejoice, and lift up your voice ;
    Shout in innocent glee
At Christmas, around the star-spangled tree.

Clap your hands in delight, and a carol indite,
    To Jesus your King ;
And Jesus will own the Hosannahs you sing.

No. II.

"When they had heard the king, they departed; and, lo, the star, which they saw in the east, went before them, till it came and stood over where the young Child was."— St. Matthew ii. 9.

BRIGHTLY stars are shining
    Over our head,
But none are so bright
    As the star which led
The shepherds of old
From midnight till morn,—
    That beautiful star,
    Which shone from afar,
In lustre like gold,
When Jesus was born.

There in a manger
Lay the sweet Stranger,
    While Bethlehem's star,
    Shining afar,
Kept watch until day
    O'er the wonderful Child,
As He peacefully lay,
By His mother caressed,
Asleep on her breast,
    The Babe undefiled.

Shining and glowing,
Where oxen are lowing,
In that manger afar,
Beautiful star !

Created to shine
On that Infant Divine !—
  Thou Heavenly Stranger,
Forsaken and lone,
  A palace Thy manger,
Thy cradle a throne !

Wise men of the age
  Are bowing before Him ;
Shepherd and sage
  Gladly adore Him :
Their offerings bring
To the new-born King ;
  Him promised of old,
The earth to redeem :
  Frankincense and gold
They proffer to Him.

And hark ! overhead
  The rustle of wings ;
Of legions outspread,
  What melody rings !
What rapturous songs,
From Angels in throngs !
  " Peace and good-will,
And God reconciled."
  O worship and kneel
To the wonderful Child !

Sing, then ! merrily sing
  Songs to the Lord !
Bells joyously ring,
  All in accord !

Children in glee,
Round the Christmas tree,
 Hail Bethlehem's star,
Which shone from afar,
 From midnight till morn,
When Jesus was born.

No. III.

"The shepherds said one to another, Let us now go even unto Bethlehem, and see this thing which is come to pass, which the Lord hath made known unto us."—St. Luke ii. 15.

Softly upon Bethlehem's plains
 Falls the gentle dew of night;
Sweetly solemn silence reigns,—
 Earth how calm, and Heaven how bright!
Every star shines out alone,
 Looking down from Heaven to earth;
Beautiful as first they shone
 Radiant at Creation's birth.

O'er the sloping mountain's side,
 Clustering flocks of sheep repose;
Watchful shepherds there abide,
 Feed and guard them from their foes:
There they watch from evening's ray,
 Sleepless until midnight's hush;
There in thoughtful musings stay,
 Till the tears of twilight gush.

Happy shepherds! lift your eyes;
 Eastward cast your glance afar;
See! what lustre gilds the skies,
 Lit by yonder signal-star!

Lyra Sabbatica.

Slow descending from above,
   See ! an Angel form appears !
God's own messenger of love
   Brings glad tidings to your ears.

See ! he folds his snowy wings ;
   Heaven in mercy stoops to earth ;
Listen to the news he brings,
   News of the Messiah's birth !
Shout in triumph, earth and Heaven,
   Swell the song of sweet accord ;
Jesus lives, " the Son is given,"
   Bow, and worship Christ the Lord.

Multitudes of Angels sing
   Strains celestial, songs Divine ;
Glory to the new-born King!
   Men may now with Angels join ;
Hallelujahs loud and long
   Swell upon the shepherds' ears,
Richer far than mortal song,
   Or the music of the spheres.

Happy shepherds ! let us go
   Unto Bethlehem and see
God made manifest below,
   Smiling on His mother's knee.
Babe Almighty ! earth's desire !
   Heaven's Anointed One art thou ;
Men and Angels, son and sire,
   Place the crown upon His brow.

CHURCH-GOING BELLS.

HERE are many rare sounds which
	fall on the ear,
	And thrill through the heart in
	sweetness and power ;
The nightingale's song, when Summer is near,
	And the blackbird and thrush just after a shower :
But as long as old England is true to her creed,
	And her Sabbaths break softly o'er mountains
	and dells,
There's no music on earth can ever exceed
	The time-hallowed tones of her church-going
	bells,
	With their delicate swells over woodlands and
	fells,
	The time-hallowed tones of her church-going
	bells.

How bright is the sunshine on Sundays ! how clear
	Is the landscape, aglow with beauty and light !
And the deep Sabbath silence, which speaks to the ear
	Of rest and devotion from morning to night !
Round the family altar what a circle is there,
	When the Bible is read and the morning hymn
	swells,
And they rise up in joy from family prayer,

To welcome the sound of the church-going bells :
So sacred yet cheering, o'er mountains and dells,
The time-hallowed voice of the church-going
bells!

O sweet 'tis to see how that magical call
Lifts the latch of the door, and throws open the
gate !
The rich and the poor, and the great and the small,
Come forth at the sound, in gladness elate ;
And grandsires, and matrons, and maidens unite,
And with groups from the school the multitude
swells ;
Dear Old England has not a more beautiful sight
Than her thousands allured by the church-going
bells,
Whose exquisite music, o'er mountains and dells,
Brings Heaven to our doors with the church-
going bells.

And often the bells ring out merry chimes,—
At weddings and christenings we love them full
well ;
And when peace follows war, and at festival times ;
And at death, ah ! how sad is the funeral knell !
But in sorrow or joy there's no echo so sweet
Can enter the house where piety dwells,
Or make the glad heart with such ecstasy beat,
As the Sabbath call of the church-going bells :
In harmony sounding o'er mountains and dells,
There's a sermon for all in the church-going bells.

When afar off the emigrant seeks for a home,
  In the lands of Old England across the broad
    seas,
Where the Saxon and Celt in the wilderness roam,
  And the axe of the woodman resounds on the
    breeze,
Soon the temple of worship uplifts its tall spire ;
  And deep in the woods, where the Englishman
    dwells,
The family altar glows with its fire,
  And the Sabbath is there, and church-going bells,
  Like music from Heaven, ring o'er mountains
    and dells,—
  O the beautiful sound of the church-going bells !

At home or abroad, in the city or town,
  In village and hamlet, or on the wild moor ;
From the palace so grand, and the Queen on the
    throne,
  To the humble and poor at the cottager's door,
The Sabbath brings blessings more precious than
    gold ;
  Our sorrows it cheers, our care it dispels ;
Pure joy to the young, and Heaven's peace to the old,
  Comes freely to all with the church-going bells.
  So God speed their echoes o'er mountains and
    dells,
  The time-honoured sound of the church-going
    bells.

THE CHURCH MILITANT.

NE with her living Head, the Church
 below
 Still journeys heavenward with her
 pilgrim train ;
Upon her forehead shines, in mystic glow,
The Cross of Baptism ; nor shines in vain
That symbol of Christ's universal reign :
Still out of Egypt, through the riven flood,
Men, women, children, from their bondage flee
To Gospel freedom, and, baptized in blood,
Are free indeed, whom Christ Himself sets free :
And through the wilderness the pillar-cloud
Shelters by day, and shields in fire by night ;
The smitten rock pours water all the way,
And manna falls, while from Mount Nebo's height
Sweet Canaan in the distance smiles in cloudless
day.

THE CHURCH TRIUMPHANT.

MIDST the sapphires on the pave-
 ment golden,
 Beyond the reach of suffering, sin,
 or woe,
Within the arms of love and mercy folden,
 Where Angels and Archangels come and go
 On high behests, and rivers softly flow,
Watering the tree of life,—triumphant, there
 The Church shall meet beneath one temple-dome,
And one eternal glow of rapture share ;
 Like children in their Father's house at home,·
Never more in the wilderness to roam ;
 With Christ for ever in full exultation,
Made like their Saviour, there to sing in bliss
 The hallelujah chorus of salvation
To Christ their Lord enthroned, and see Him as
 He is.

Printed by J. and W. Rider, 14, Bartholomew Close, London.

www.ingramcontent.com/pod-product-compliance
Lightning Source LLC
Chambersburg PA
CBHW030556040726
47497CB00008B/2748